ROCKED by
GOD

ROCKED by
GOD

a mom's true story of suffering, surrender, and survival after medical trauma

TIFFANY STROUD

This book is dedicated to my mom—for holding me with open hands to allow God to work in my life and for helping strengthen my foundation from a young age so I would be prepared for the earthquakes of life.

And to Raylee, Ruthi, and Josiah—may you be rocked by God in every way possible.

Contents

Introduction

The thief comes only to steal and kill and
destroy; I have come that they may have life
and have it to the full.

John 10:10

"I want to move you to the ICU," Dr. Ali said. His deep brown eyes
moved from the chart in his hand to me. "I know that sounds
scary, but this is going to be the best option for you. You'll get
the best care. This is what I would recommend if you were my
own sister."

That's the last thing I remember. I don't remember being
wheeled into the ICU room. I don't remember meeting the nurse.
I don't remember being on the BiPap machine or that it didn't
work. I definitely don't remember when they asked my husband
for permission to intubate me and put me on a ventilator. Or did
they ask me? I have no idea. I don't remember a room full of visitors bringing me balloons and singing me happy birthday.

I do remember a few things, though. There were people with
me—namely my husband, Travis, who barely left my side. One
memory I do have is an embarrassing one of drooling on my
father-in-law's shoes and wondering why–not realizing how sig-
nificant it was that I was standing while on life support.

But much of my memory has been erased from those days in the hospital. It's a mix of trauma, sickness, and sedation. Together, they left me with bits and pieces of memories.

Eventually I grew tired of asking questions all the time and finding out what happened to me. I'd ask, "Why didn't they do surgery?" or "When did they decide to intubate me?"

So, one day, while our daughters napped, Travis helped me piece together the full story. We sat on our gray bedspread in our home in Louisville, Kentucky and worked through the full timeline. He searched back into the group texts to reread his updates to family. He reread his Facebook posts from when he began to update the world on my condition. I wrote it all down: the words doctors said or didn't say; my heart rate and white blood cell count; the possibilities of another surgery; and his responses to it all. I looked over the notes my mom had written down and the list of all the visitors who came, many of whom I didn't remember.

When I had a breathing tube down my throat, I couldn't talk. So I scratched out notes on blank paper to communicate. We looked through those too. He pointed to one where I had written PUNCH in all caps across the paper, explaining that I wrote it right after my surly surgeon left the room. He showed me where I drew the tiniest picture of a cat, which somehow meant, "How are the girls?" By girls, I'm not talking about cats. We didn't even own a cat, so I am clueless as to how he eventually figured out that I wanted to know how our daughters were doing. I'm not quite sure how he figured out much of what those scratches meant. I don't even recognize my own handwriting. Sometimes it was tiny and overlapping. Other times I wrote in big bold letters, taking up half the paper.

Together with my husband on that day, I reread the text I sent my friend Becky who showed up at the hospital while I was newly intubated. *Sorry Becky Thayer I Hahn Irene n ram nexas. Nexsksss. Xand sand deskj Wifn tnjd through thbr in!* I do remember thinking I was texting, *Sorry I didn't get to talk to you much but thanks for coming.*

As if she needed an apology that I couldn't talk to her, not that she could understand any of what I wanted to say anyway.

When we had the whole timeline assembled, I sat back and looked at it all. But it didn't bring the memories back to me. There are still black gaps, blank spaces in my brain—hours, days, memories I'll never get back. And maybe that's good. Perhaps that's another example of God's compassion toward me. I imagine, from what I know now, I wouldn't want those missing pieces of my story intact. Maybe the sedation that stole my memories was in fact a gift from God—another one of the ways He took care of me through some of the greatest suffering I've ever experienced.

In the pages of this book is my story of survival. I survived sepsis, a condition that kills eight million people each year, according to the National Institutes of Health. I walked away without any amputations—something that many can't say. I somehow made a complete physical recovery in an abnormally short amount of time. I didn't only heal physically. This is also the story of my journey to heal mentally and emotionally. I would work through Post Traumatic Stress Disorder (PTSD) and Post Intensive Care Syndrome (PICS) for years, and I would slowly but surely mentally heal from my ordeal. As I went through Eye Movement Desensitization and Reprocessing (EMDR) therapy, I came to realize simple truths that weaved through each memory I still had. Common themes that showed up in my own story even though much of it was told to me like a child being told a bedtime story.

Even though I had little or no control over my experience, God was with me and took care of me in each moment. I was never alone—even when the visitors went back to the waiting room, even when the nurses went back to their stations, and even when my family finally convinced my husband to run home to shower or walk across the street for some non-hospital food.

As a self-proclaimed control freak who wants to be in charge of every detail, finding myself in a state of helplessness was hard to swallow. (Actually it was literally impossible to swallow—being on a ventilator and all.) But as I worked through the memories and details, I learned that I didn't need that control. Even in my helplessness, God was taking care of each detail, each piece of the story. He was taking care of me in a thousand different ways, through my family, in little miracles like my five-month-old taking a bottle (which she had refused previously) when I couldn't breastfeed anymore, and a complete stranger who showed up when I needed an angel.

As the years passed, the ways God was taking care of me through this whole ordeal became clearer and clearer. Someone once called me "a living breathing testimony to God's healing power" and with a title like that, I feel obligated to share that story. He didn't do all this just for my good or even to answer the many prayers that were lifted up into the great beyond on my behalf. I believe He did it for you. Because God's telling me to share this story, it must mean that He wants you to hear it.

Maybe He wants you to know He can heal. Maybe He wants you to know that He hears you. Maybe He wants you to know you aren't alone. I believe He wants you to know He will take care of you. That no matter what terrible situation you've been through or are going through, He's got you in His hands. And He's not letting go.

Because He heard me. He healed me. He was with me. He took care of me and still is. I'm in His hands and nothing and nobody can pluck me from that spot. I hope as you read my story, you'll feel that is true for yourself as well. I hope this book reveals missing pieces to you about your own story—pieces that show that God was with you all along even when He felt silent. Because I've been in that place too—the place of unanswered prayers.

Although I've learned that I was never alone and that God was taking care of me every step of the way, one of the biggest parts to my trauma was how I couldn't take care of my children.

I can't remember a time I didn't want to be a mom. I loved being "mom" when playing house as a child. When we got older, my cousins and I would climb out their bedroom window to sit on the roof and chat about what we wanted to name our future children while we looked at the stars in the night sky. I'd write my name ideas in my notebook, practicing the lettering and trying out different spellings. Joshua, Skylar, Reagan . . .

When the question was asked, "What do you want to be when you grow up?" many different careers came up like singer or hotel manager, but the one job title that never changed: mom. It felt like a calling God had placed within my heart.

In college, I babysat a lot for extra money. Since I loved caring for young kids, I took a couple jobs at churches to help with childcare. I'll never forget little Eli with his plump rosy cheeks and blonde hair. He was almost two, and I saw him twice a week while his mom went to a Bible study at two different churches. I remember when his mom would come to pick him up from the church nurseries. The way he would run to her with the biggest smile on his face, yelling, "mama!" My heart burst at the sight of him rushing to her and the sound of his little voice proclaiming her as his own. One day, he fell and busted his lip. I felt chosen and needed when he ran past another childcare worker and into my arms. I knew I wanted that someday.

When I was first admitted to the hospital, two sweet little girls called me "mama." Well, technically just one, since Ruthi couldn't talk yet. She was only five months old. But Raylee was two and had that precious toddler voice that made your heart swell when she said "mama." They were mine. I was theirs.

I took on most of the responsibility when raising them simply because my husband worked outside the home, and I stayed home with them. I planned and cooked meals and bought snacks at the grocery store. I cleaned up the spills and calmed the meltdowns. Sometimes I disciplined to teach the lesson, and sometimes I tickled to hear the giggles. I put them down for their naps, built block towers with them, and kissed their boo-boos. I picked out their clothes and dressed them, changed diapers, potty trained . . . you get the idea. I was *the* mom.

And then I found myself struggling for my own life in the hospital, completely helpless, powerless to take care of my children or even see them. I felt like my role of mama—a role I'd had for only two years at this point—was stripped from me. I wasn't the one taking care of them anymore. I was the one being taken care of. It was a change I was not prepared for.

Being out of control like that rocked me and left me with a paralyzing fear. What would happen to my children if I never came home? It was a fear that ate away at me long after I left the hospital and moved into everyday life. I remember one time holding back panic attacks as our airplane hit turbulence while we flew off to an adventure without our children. I pictured someone telling my kids their parents weren't coming home. I could see the confusion and sorrow in their little blue eyes. I would think of how that day would haunt them for the rest of their lives, how it would change their hearts forever.

Years after my trauma, an anxiety disorder led me to spiral into thoughts about terrible situations that could happen to my kids. I'd lay awake while the rest of the house was asleep playing out the scenario of accidently crashing into a body of water. I'd try to save them all before they drowned as our car submerged into the rushing waters, but the nightmare would never end. I could never figure out how to save them all. The scene felt so real and so intense that I'd lie there crying, unable to sleep. Another night I pictured one of them lost in the woods, alone and petrified, while the sun began to set, and I desperately searched for them to no avail.

This story is not only about how God took care of me. It's also the story of how God took care of my children when I couldn't. How He taught me that He will take care of them no matter what happens to me. And if you're a mama too, I can guarantee you have similar fears for your children. Maybe you aren't picturing them drowning, but you have your own nightmares.

We all have fears that eat away at us. I bet you worry about your children as much as I worry about mine. You worry about their bodies being injured or coming down with illness. You worry about their hearts being broken or the losses and tragedies that will come throughout their lives. You worry about what would happen to them if something happened to you, and you feel the weight of being the mom, the lead role in caring for them.

I bet if for nothing else, God wants me to write this to show you that you aren't the only one rocking those babies in the middle of the night. He holds them first because they belong to Him, not us. He holds them when we can't.

I believe even when we *can* hold them and take care of them, He's holding *us* in His hands the whole time. When we finally learn that and let go of our need for control, we can surrender our children to the One we can fully trust. I must constantly remind myself of this truth, because you don't trust God once, although I wish it were that easy. Trusting God is a daily task of surrender. It's choosing to put our full weight on Him, even when we don't feel like it. But the more we do it, the less pressure and anxiety we will feel.

Surrendering to God and trusting Him are the missing pieces when it comes to finding full peace, not just as a mama, but simply as a daughter of the King. Some days, it's the only way to survive. You may not be in a hospital bed. Maybe you've never experienced medical trauma. But no matter what you've been through or where you are now, I hope that my story shows you that God is worthy of our trust. That you, your children, and even your unanswered prayers are safe in His hands.

PART 1

Suffering

CHAPTER 1

Hospital Angel

For he will command his angels concerning you
to guard you in all your ways.

Psalm 91:11

It all began in January 2020. I finished cleaning out our basement storage closet. You know, the one that you throw random items into—totes of outgrown clothes, the box of Christmas ornaments, the beach toys that you only need in the summer. Suddenly you can't walk into the closet anymore. It felt refreshing to pull everything out, purge what we didn't need, and reorganize all the items still inside. We could walk all the way in and find whatever we needed now.

I love being organized. Clutter and mess make me feel out of control. And I like control. Even though it can sometimes be intimidating or overwhelming, being the one holding all the responsibility gives me assurance. Because I can trust myself best. Other people may let me down or mess up, but if I'm in charge, I feel like all will be okay.

Once the closest project was complete, our Christmas break

was over. Travis went back to work, and I went back to caring for Raylee and Ruthi. We got back into our routine of Travis going to work in the mornings while I handled everything at home. I enjoyed the role of a stay-at-home mom because I didn't have to trust anyone else with my babies. I had the sole duty of protecting and caring for them. Just like an organization project, I had the control. The closet was in my hands. My kids were in my hands.

It was a normal Saturday in the middle of the night. I was awake to breastfeed Ruthi. She was waking up about once a night for a feeding at that point, and the girl refused to take a bottle—a problem we had with Raylee as well, so we were used to it. I leaned my head back against the chair while she fed and noticed a deep ache in my stomach. I moved to lessen the pain but didn't worry too much about it. I was too tired, and as soon as she was back to sleep, so was I.

Early the next morning, I was up for her next feeding, but now the dull ache had grown into a constant cramping. I could tell it was my lower abdomen that felt the pain. I figured it was gas, but once she was done with her feeding, I brought her to Travis and told him I didn't feel good. We stayed home from church that morning so I could stay in bed all day. Travis took care of the girls and brought Ruthi to me whenever she was ready to eat. I thought for sure it must be constipation or gas and that I'd be fine the next day.

But by late Monday afternoon, I crawled up the stairs instead of walking because of the gnawing pain in my abdomen. I decided at that point that I would go to urgent care that evening. I didn't think it was anything actually urgent though, so I drove myself there after we put the girls to bed. By the time I got to urgent care, I was bent over holding my stomach.

It hurt worse to walk, and just my luck, the parking lot was so full that I had to park at the end of the lot and walk much further. Once I got into an exam room, I was shivering so much that a nurse wrapped a blanket around me and asked me to lay down.

The doctor came in a few moments later and asked me the

standard questions. But his face grew somber when I told him how long I'd been experiencing this pain in my abdomen.

"You need to go to the ER," he told me after pushing on my stomach.

Naïve that this could be serious, I asked, "Does it have to be tonight, or could I wait and go tomorrow?"

"You definitely need to go tonight," he said. "There are so many things it could be with your abdomen—your ovaries, your appendix, your intestines. I could run all kinds of tests, and I'd still end up sending you to the ER."

My mind raced. I didn't want to take Ruthi to the hospital, but she wouldn't take a bottle. *How long would I have to wait at the ER? Would it go past her nightly feeding? How would she eat without me?*

I called Travis right away and shared my distress. We decided our only option was to take Ruthi with us so I could feed her when she needed to eat. We called my mom, who lived three hours away, to be on stand-by in case we would need her to come take care of the girls for us. We didn't have any family nearby. We asked our neighbor who had two teenage daughters if they could come over to our house to keep an eye on the monitor while Raylee slept. I was the typical mom who was more worried about my babies than I was about myself.

In the ER, I was taken back for a CT scan. I had never done this before. My hands were shaky and my heart was racing. My brother, who happened to work in a hospital as a cardiac CATH lab technologist, explained through text what to expect.

"It's going to feel like you peed your pants," he said. And he was exactly right. The nurse told me she was putting the contrast into my IV. A warm sensation came over me. I was glad I had been warned because it really did feel like I was peeing. The machine surrounding me began to whir, and I focused on breathing so I wouldn't panic.

The nurses said it could be two hours before we found out the results, but surprisingly someone came in within ten minutes.

"It's your appendix," he said. "It's the biggest appendix I've ever seen. It definitely has to come out. We're going to call the surgeon and schedule surgery."

I was shocked. *Surgery? I don't do well with medical stuff. That CT scan was enough for me. Are we sure we need to do this?*

The doctor calmed me down with a simple explanation. Appendicitis happens when an appendix becomes diseased and swollen because it's been filled with mucus, stool, or parasites. It's common—and removing an appendix is a routine and common surgery. My uncle had an appendectomy the week before and was back to work in two days.

We called my mom to ask her to come and my surgery was scheduled for the next morning. But by then the wracking pain made me want to rip out my abdomen. I wasn't scared of the surgery anymore. All I wanted was to get it over with! Especially since I declined the pain medication to protect Ruthi while I breastfed. The things we endure for our children!

As a nurse wheeled me back to the operating room and helped move me to the operating table, I sighed in relief. When I woke up, I'd be pain-free.

But when my eyes fluttered open only an hour later, my entire torso from the chest down past my waist ached like the worst stomachache. There was no chance of getting up out of that bed soon. I would lift my head, and the nurse would place a few ice chips in my mouth. I'd lay my head back down, dozing in and out of consciousness.

I stayed in that recovery room surrounded by curtain walls that separated me from the other patients coming out of surgery for longer than normal. But this didn't cause anyone any concern. The doctor signed off to release me later that day, and I hoped I'd return to normal soon. I was told recovery would only take a couple days. Soon I could get back to my day-to-day life playing with Raylee and changing diapers for Ruthi. Except, I didn't. For a week, I woke up each morning as the ache in my lower stomach grew worse. The searing pain made it difficult to do much of anything but lay in bed.

Thankfully, many friends from church and family volunteered to come to my house during my "recovery" after surgery. Katy brought her three young children over to play with Raylee. She spent the whole day at my house, changing Ruthi's diapers, cleaning my kitchen, and getting me anything I needed as I rested. I was astounded that she would serve me, despite her own busy life with three littles.

A week after my surgery, my Aunt Traci stayed overnight with us to help as I fully expected to take over my mom duties again. I was ready to get back to normal. I went to put Ruthi down for her nap, rocking her in the gray glider in her room. But as soon as I stood up, uncontrollable diarrhea soiled my sweatpants. I stood in shock, holding my baby. What was happening? I called out to my aunt for help and felt thankful she was staying with us rather than a friend from church. I would've felt so embarrassed.

I told her what happened and let her take over putting Ruthi down for her nap while I cleaned myself up. I seemed to have no control over my bowels at all anymore. I felt embarrassed and gross. I was incapable of doing much knowing it could happen again at any moment.

After a week and a half of not recovering as expected, I called my surgeon's office multiple times. "I'm still in a lot of pain," I said to the nurse over the phone.

"Do you have a fever?"

"No, but I'm having uncontrollable diarrhea."

"That can be normal," she said. "If you don't have a fever, I wouldn't worry. Just wait until your follow-up appointment."

But by day 12 of "recovery," I hit a level of pain that I couldn't take anymore.

For days, I ate according to the BRAT diet—bananas, rice, applesauce, or toast—to try to stop my uncontrollable diarrhea. I was barely eating anything, but it didn't help. One night, I finally said, "Forget it." I wanted to eat something I actually liked.

We ordered take out from a well-known BBQ restaurant in Louisville. It was the first restaurant we had ever tried while visiting the city to look at houses. I didn't know it at the time, but it would also be the last time I'd eat their BBQ. Not because the food caused the next hospital stay, but because their signature savory taste will forever trigger memories of the night my life changed.

We put the girls to bed and went down to our basement to eat and watch TV. I was thankful to finally eat something other than a banana. When I was finished, I set the takeout box on the coffee table in front of me and texted with a friend who was telling me the awesome news she was pregnant. As we were texting, I rubbed my stomach as it began to ache more and more. I'd been in pain for almost two weeks now, but in that moment the pain amped up like never before.

"Ugh, maybe I shouldn't have eaten that," I said.

"Tiff, you should be able to eat," Travis said in frustration.

I thought maybe I needed to go to the bathroom. I set my phone down, but my stomach felt like it was being eaten from the inside out. I couldn't walk. I thought maybe I'd just crawl to the bathroom. But I didn't even make it halfway. I was on the floor with my hands and knees, clutching my stomach.

"Something's not right," I said to Travis. "You're right. It shouldn't be this bad. Call someone to watch the girls."

Travis grabbed my phone and began making calls. I was going through my list of friends too—most of whom had their own kids to take care of. They couldn't leave them in the middle of the night for my kids, and all of our family members were three hours away. Then I thought of Tressella. She was like a mentor or bonus grandma that I had met at church. She and her husband were retired, and I knew she'd come if I needed her. Travis called them, and they left immediately.

Travis helped me up the stairs and onto the couch, abandoning the takeout box on the coffee table. I wonder who ended up throwing it away. How long did it sit there? He put my shoes on me and began to pack a small bag—a change of clothes and our phone chargers.

"Make a bottle," I said in a whisper. He got a bottle ready for

Tressella to use in the middle of the night. Only a few days earlier, when I didn't feel like I was recovering from the surgery, I weaned Ruthi from the breast. It felt upsetting at the time, to think of putting myself before my daughter, letting go of feeding her the way she was used to so that I could take care of myself. But now I know it was another way God was taking care of each little detail. I can't imagine if I had developed mastitis—an infection that can occur when your breasts get too full of milk and clog—during my hospital stay.

Thankfully, this night, Ruthi was already taking bottles well. Travis showed Tressella and her husband how to work our baby monitor and how to heat the pre-made bottle of formula. I could tell they were worried about me since I could barely walk or talk at that point. They said they were praying as Travis helped me wobble into the car.

Travis rushed me to the ER, even running a red light. I rated my pain level a nine, which even surprised me. This was worse than my appendicitis. I kept asking for pain medicine, but they would only offer me morphine. I knew from a previous medical trauma that my body couldn't handle morphine. It sent me into what I consider a coma. I could hear and understand everything around me, but I couldn't open my eyes, talk, or even squeeze my fingers. I felt trapped in my own body, so scared and confused. I never wanted to experience that again. But now, with pain racking my body, I was desperate.

"Just give me the morphine," I said to the nurse.

Turning to Travis, I said with a shaking voice, "Just remember: I'm still here. If it does what it did last time, I can still hear you. I won't be able to respond. I won't be able to move at all."

The nurses started the morphine into my IV and my blood pressure tanked, exactly like before. They stopped it immediately. I wanted to yell, "Told you so!" but instead I was trying to stay alert, prying my eyes open, and praying that somehow this pain would lessen. The nurses gave me some other type of medicine, but it didn't touch the pain.

A CT scan easily located the problem: a massive infection inside my abdomen, caused by the appendicitis. Doctors think my appendix had seeped bacteria into my abdomen before it was removed. I was admitted, and we called my mom to come be with the girls once again. The next morning, a doctor put in a drain—a procedure I do not remember. All I do remember is seeing a rectangle shaped bag attached to my abdomen, disgusting, yellow-colored liquid oozing out of me. A nurse later told me they knew I had a severe infection by the amount of puss that had gushed out.

"No wonder you were in so much pain," she said.

They had emptied out 400 milliliters, which is almost two cups, of infected puss from my abdomen. But even with the removed liquid, the gnawing pain in my stomach was constant. It felt like it was moving into my lower chest, and now I was having trouble catching my breath. I told the nurse, but she wasn't concerned. When my surgeon came to check on me, I told him my concern. He too said to not worry. It was because of the gas used to put in the drain—perfectly normal.

My mom called later in the day, and I was trying to give her instructions on what to pack for the kids so she could take them to my mother-in-law. My mom needed to go back to work. She had already taken time off to be with us during my surgery. But while on the phone with her, I was having such a hard time catching my breath, I could hardly talk. It felt exhausting, and I gave up, handing the phone to Travis and pointing to the packing list I keep in my Notes app for trips. He copied and pasted the list and sent it to my mom. I felt relieved knowing the girls would have everything they needed, except their mama, of course.

Two of Travis's aunts, Rhonda and Laura, are nurses, and news of my condition spread fast. Both called or texted to check on me, and both were concerned with my breathing difficulty. They told us to keep bringing it up and keep asking questions because something didn't sound right.

Enter: my Hospital Angel. I didn't call her that at the time. She would get that nickname from me later. She had straight brown hair that came down to her shoulders. She walked with confidence like she not only enjoyed her job, but she was good at it and knew it—not in a cocky way, though. She was part of the Interventional Radiology (IR) team that put my drain in. They were checking on their patients with drains.

She walked into my room and reviewed my chart. The doctor and nurse had ignored me, maybe she would listen. I told her how I couldn't catch my breath. She grew concerned—the first person at the hospital to do so. I explained what my surgeon had said.

"He said it was normal because . . . of the gas you use to . . . put the drain in," I said with a question in my tone between breaths.

"We don't use gas to put a drain in," she said, eyebrows furrowing. "That's not normal at all."

My face grew hot and my jaw tensed. *How did my surgeon not know what a drain procedure was like?* I could see Travis's eyes flash in anger as well, and his concern for me grew as his forehead creased.

My Hospital Angel told me my oxygen levels were at 93 when they should have been at 99. She put me on oxygen and ordered a chest X-ray. She set into motion all the steps needed to save me from dying that day, because I would later find out that my respiratory rate was so low, my heart would have given out soon. I didn't even have twenty-four hours. I probably would have died before my surgeon made his next rounds.

She was the first person on the medical staff to seriously listen to me. I never did figure out my Hospital Angel's real name. In the years since, I've tried to find her with no luck. But I'll never forget her, that's for sure. And this wasn't the last time I'd see her because my hospital visit was far from over.

CHAPTER 2

Rocked by God

And he said to her, "Daughter, your faith has
healed you. Go in peace and be freed from
your suffering."

Mark 5:34

I remember my pulmonologist, Dr. Ali. He was the second doctor
to take on my case. Eventually four doctors—a surgeon, pulmonologist, the hospitalist, and an infectious disease doctor—saw me.
Dr. Ali, with his brown eyes and white coat, was the most person-
able of the four. Even though I only remember talking to him one
time, he became my favorite. After all, he was the one who took
my case the most earnestly.

He told us that the chest X-ray showed fluid in my lungs. They
began medication to relieve the fluid while reducing the fluids
coursing through my IV. But the oxygen and breathing treatments
weren't enough at that point. When I got up to go to the bathroom,
which was only a few steps away, my oxygen rate dropped to 82
and my heart rate went up to 140. Somehow, I was getting worse.

"I want to move you to the ICU," Dr. Ali said. "I know that

sounds scary, but this is going to be the best option for you. You'll get the best care. This is what I would recommend if you were my own sister."

The words rang in my ear and the team moved quickly, rushing me to more specialized care. It would be a week before I'd begin to learn how desperately I needed it, but Travis was soon to discover what we were facing.

Travis called my mom to tell her I was being moved to the ICU. Later, she would tell me that she had just dumped her clothes out of her duffle bag after arriving home from dropping our girls off with my mother-in-law, Mary Jo. My mom said, "I'm on my way."

She scooped up her clothes and threw them back in the bag. She rushed to tell my dad, who was working outside with a friend. Leaving as fast as she could, she didn't even realize she hadn't grabbed her socks and underwear from the pile of clothes on her bed. Little did she know it would be four of the longest weeks of her life before she'd get back home.

In the ICU, nurses tried more breathing treatments and a BiPAP machine to improve my breathing. But it only continued to worsen. Fluid still puddled in my lungs, but that wasn't the worst of our problems. The real reason for my labored breathing was because the pain had moved up into my diaphragm. It hurt too much to take a breath.

Dr. Ali decided to put me on a ventilator—a machine that would breathe for me. You probably know of it as "life support." Without the ventilator, Dr. Ali didn't think I would survive the night.

Travis and I looked at each other. He told me that he loved me and I'd be okay. The nurses assured him he did not want to be in the room during the procedure, and that the best, most experienced doctor would intubate me. I kissed him goodbye. He left the room and began relaying this new turn of events to family.

Two hours into my mom's drive, her phone rang again.

"I need to prepare you," Travis said to her. "They just put her on a ventilator."

It suddenly became the longest drive of my mom's life as she desperately tried to get to me safely, despite the tears clouding her view. Her memories of taking her father-in-law off of life support terrified her about what may lie ahead.

She called my dad right away, who was just leaving to come to the hospital. Because it was so late, he spent the night in a hotel. I have no idea how hard that drive and night alone must have been for my dad. He arrived at the hospital early the next morning, just an hour before my brother and his wife arrived too.

When Travis came back to my room that night after making phone calls, I was sedated, a tube down my throat, unable to talk even if I were awake. The weight of our situation crashed onto him. He felt shocked and confused, unable to comprehend what was happening. It had all happened so fast. As he stared at me lying on the hospital bed, almost lifeless, loneliness filled the room.

But he wasn't alone. None of us ever were. God was taking care of him, because only minutes went by before Nathan showed up. Nathan was a church friend who happened to be near the hospital at that exact time. His wife had found out at that evening's Wednesday night service about my situation. News spread fast as people asked for prayers.

When Nathan found out, he grabbed dinner for Travis and came to the hospital. I don't know what they talked about or if they even talked at all. But God made sure Travis knew he was not alone at that moment. Nathan was another husband and father standing beside him. He represented an entire church family supporting us and lifting us up in prayer. He was the first visitor of dozens.

"She has a condition called sepsis," Paige, the ICU nurse, told Travis. Travis nodded. He wasn't surprised. His aunts, Laura and Rhonda, had already explained to him what sepsis is since they believed I was going septic when I had trouble breathing.

I had never heard the term before my hospital stay. A lot of people think it's an infection of the blood, but that's not the case. Sepsis is a condition where your body overreacts to an infection, according to Sepsis Alliance, which is an organization that I would learn so much from about a year later.

Sepsis damages vital organs and can lead to death. It's a medical emergency like a heart attack or stroke, but for some reason it's not as well known. Our immune systems fight off germs like bacteria and viruses to prevent infections. When we do get an infection, our bodies will continue trying to fight it off. Many times, we need some type of medication like antibiotics to help fight the infection. But sometimes—and researchers haven't figured out why yet—our immune systems turn on themselves and begin to fight our bodies rather than the infections. This is the start of sepsis, which can progress to severe sepsis.

The signs of severe sepsis are organ dysfunction, like difficulty breathing, not peeing enough, or mental decline. This can then progress to septic shock, the worst stage, where your blood pressure drops dangerously low. Many survivors end up with amputations because of the poor blood flow or where their infection began. Any type of infection can lead to sepsis—strep throat, a tiny cut on your finger, or a urinary tract infection, to name a few.

My condition worsened as they tried to keep me stable over the next few days. My infectious disease doctor frantically ran test after test, trying to find the right antibiotic to treat the infection inside my abdomen. Many of our family members visited. They sat with Travis, asked the nurses questions, and held my hand. People sent or brought flowers, and our family set pictures of my daughters up where I could see them. Looking back at the list of people who came to the hospital while I was in that ICU bed, I feel incredibly loved. But it also makes me realize how bad my condition was. I wonder if those family members came to say goodbye.

Many people asked what they could do to help us during our crisis. The number one answer was always prayer. Our family asked everyone to pray. A photo of me with little blond Raylee and newborn Ruthi with her dark head of hair was shared on social media with a plea for prayers.

Other than prayers, the second answer was to support Tra-

vis's youngest sister, Cara, and her husband, Justin, as they kept
Raylee and Ruthi for us. Both sets of grandparents worked, but
Cara stayed home with her babies, so she was available to watch
our kids. Cara and Justin had their own three children to care for,
which meant they already had tons of toys and baby supplies. It
was a perfect set up for the girls, but it also meant Cara and Justin
cared for five children, all two years old and younger. There's
another miracle in this story: the fact that *they* survived!

Cara and Justin had moved from South Carolina to Indiana to
be near family six months before this. Of course, God had many
plans and purposes for their family to be there. But I can't help
but think that He orchestrated that move just in time for them
to step in as caregivers for our girls when they suddenly were, in
a sense, orphans. Did God set that in motion knowing we would
desperately need them?

Travis and I will always be grateful that they took on the huge
task of caring for our girls, not knowing how long I'd be in the
hospital. Cara and I had become especially close in that past year.

We had visited often while Travis and his other sister opened a
coffee roastery and cafe in his hometown in Indiana, three hours
away from our house. We would stay with Cara and Justin whenever we visited, so our girls were used to their home. A Pack 'n
Play and diaper changing pad was set up in one bedroom with
a toddler-sized bed assembled in another area of the basement.

Our kids played well together too. Raylee and her cousin,
Luca, who are just over two months apart in age, are the very
best of friends. Cara and I worked together well whenever we
stayed with them, taking turns doing chores around the house.
We shared tasks like cooking or folding laundry, always willing
to help each other. Cara and I spent many nights up late talking
while our husbands played video games together, or all four of us
would play board games after the kids went to bed. They quickly
became some of our closest friends during those visits, and we
often joked about how fun it would be to live together all the time.

I can't imagine how hard those weeks were for Cara while I was in the hospital. I imagine her blond hair pulled into a bun on top of her head and her blue eyes struggling to stay awake after too many nights of not enough sleep. To know you could lose your friend, to not be able to come to the hospital with other family members, to think of your brother becoming a widower, and to look into the eyes of those little girls knowing their mama might not ever come get them. *How did Cara do that day in and day out?*

As I've gotten to know Cara more as the years have passed, she has become my best friend. Now I know how she did it: she leans into God. She leans into the support of her family, and I know Justin was caring for her while she was giving so much of herself to the kids all day. I'm sure it didn't hurt that she's incredibly strong, independent, and determined. If she wanted to climb Mount Everest, she would. I have no doubts. (It's what makes her an incredible accountability partner for my workouts.)

Many family members brought Cara's family meals, snacks, and stopped by to give her a break. They helped me by helping her.

While the girls were taken care of three hours north, I was in the ICU about to "celebrate" my birthday. It was my last day of being thirty years old. I love my birthday and getting to celebrate. I had planned to get an expensive pedicure—something I only do about four times a year—then go shopping with my mom, one of our favorite pastimes even if it's just to window shop and dream.

Most of all, I expected to eat cake. I'm a total sweet tooth. My favorite food is ice cream, but I'll never turn down a cookie or a piece of cake, especially if chocolate is involved. But this birthday was about to look a lot different than I had expected.

My feet weren't wrapped in warm towels or being rubbed by hot stones. They were wrapped in hospital socks with grips on the bottoms—not that I was doing any walking. The only shopping was someone stopping at the downstairs gift shop to buy me a travel pillow to help hold my head up so I wouldn't get a kink in my neck while sedated.

And cake? It was out of the question. You can't eat cake with a tube down your throat. In fact, by my birthday they hadn't even put a feeding tube in yet. I hadn't eaten anything in days. Instead, Travis would take a little stick with a sponge on the end, dip it in water, and rub it around my mouth to ease the dryness. Sometimes, I'd point at that stick, craving it like a desert explorer with an empty canteen.

The CT scan I had that morning showed the infection had spread to my ovary. The infectious disease doctor hadn't found the correct antibiotic for all the different types of bacteria growing inside me.

My abdominal pain split through me, as little pockets of infection swam all throughout my abdomen and torso. Surgery was discussed as I had laid in the bed practically lifeless all day. Should they go in and remove as much of the infection as they could? Should they take out my ovary?

Surgery was always a possibility, so I had to stay on the ventilator in case they needed to operate. But the truth was, they didn't think I'd survive the surgery. Even if I did, I'd have an open wound, a long gaping hole from my chest down my torso and through my abdomen. The wound would need to close on its own. The recovery would be massive. My blood pressure was too low, and my body, too weak. The surgeon had said that morning that he didn't advise surgery because he didn't believe I would survive it.

But later that evening, the hospitalist came in to review my chart. He told my family they would do the surgery to remove as much of the infection as they could, even removing my ovary. My mom began crying, almost hysterical as her fears swirled in her head and spilled out through her emotions leaving her in a panic.

"Kristy, stop," Kendall, my sister-in-law, said sternly into my mom's face. She went into nurse mode (her job in Indianapolis) and would not let my mom's dark thoughts pull her under. "She's not dying. We are not going there. We are not going to think that way until we have a reason to think that way."

Tim, my father-in-law and a physical therapist, calmly agreed. "The hospitalist is not the one who makes the final decision on whether we do surgery or not."

Their words helped calm my mom, but nerves were high. I never ended up having surgery to remove the infection, but it was always a possibility–always a scary prospect that lurked around the corner.

Things got worse that night, a fever hit my body, and my heart rate dropped. Everyone began to realize that I may not make it through the night.

My mom went to the waiting room and called my Aunt Traci, who had called earlier in the day to see if she could come visit. My mom had told her to just wait until tomorrow since it was already late in the afternoon and such a long drive. Now, my mom kept thinking that if I didn't make it through the night, she would regret telling Traci to wait.

"I think you need to come," my mom said, holding in tears.

"I'm already on my way," said Traci. "I was going to come and stay in a hotel tonight, but I'll just come straight to the hospital now."

Others had headed to the waiting room of the hospital too, while some headed to our house to sleep for the night. Travis and I were alone in the room when one of the doctors came in for an update. Travis followed him out of my room. He thought he was ready to hear the truth from the doctor. But he wasn't ready, because whoever is?

"How serious is this?" Travis asked. "What are her chances?"

"It's very serious," the doctor replied, hesitating. "Her chances are 50/50."

Travis collapsed at the news. He began sobbing as nurses and the doctor pulled him off to a side room. He wept. I imagine he was picturing telling our two-year-old her mama was not coming home—a thought he had been pushing away for as long as possible. Travis didn't want to be away from me for too long, so he pulled himself together and came back to my room.

He laid down on his makeshift bed, crying and thinking about how he wouldn't be able to sleep that night. He couldn't stop thinking of having to raise our daughters without me, and he wasn't sure how he could hold strong to his faith in such a heartbreaking situation. Hot tears of anger and heartbreak rolled down his cheeks.

It was quiet—as quiet as a hospital can be. Beeps, footsteps, the drip of the IV. The lights were low, the room dark except for all the machines keeping me alive.

Suddenly, the lights in the room began to slowly brighten and then dim again. Back and forth the lighting went—bright, dim, bright, dim. When he looked up at me on my hospital bed, surrounded by all the tubes and wires, he saw that my knees were bent with my feet still on the bed. My legs were slowly rocking back and forth. Ever since we'd been moved to this room, my movements were always rigid, painful. My movements in this moment were different—gentle.

It was at that instant that Travis felt peace wash over him. He felt God's presence like never before and knew, without a doubt, no matter what happened, everything was going to be okay. He happened to look up at the clock. It was 9:02 p.m. He suddenly remembered that a prayer vigil had been set for 9 p.m. that night. Travis's Aunt Rhonda had the idea of a prayer vigil and started spreading the word, asking people to pray for me at that exact time. During her prayers that night, she was specifically praying that God would rock me in His arms. Travis knew people were praying for me at that exact moment.

He had no idea how many people, though. Of course, he knew our families and lots of friends were praying. But social media had spread the news, and we found out later that people from all over were praying for me—church groups in other states, friends of friends, even families as far away as Thailand.

I rocked back and forth while sedated as the lights danced for fifteen minutes. I believe I was rocked by God. Like a loving parent comforting their sick baby in the middle of the dark night. I believe God was hearing those prayers, and He was healing me.

I now picture myself small and weak cradled in his large, strong hands. I picture Him calling me "daughter" and telling me everything is going to be okay—the same way I would hold my own babies whispering, "It's okay. Mama's here. You're okay."

I know I was being healed that night while God rocked me because it was the very next day—my birthday—that I began to improve for the first time since coming to the hospital.

CHAPTER 3

Birthday Cake

So do not fear, for I am with you; be not
dismayed, for I am your God. I will strengthen
you and help you; I will uphold you with my
righteous right hand.

Isaiah 41:10

It was my thirty-first birthday. I am told I had many visitors that day, but those twenty-four hours don't even exist in my memory. It gives me the chance to joke that I get to stay thirty! I don't remember anyone singing to me, but I'm told a room full of people sang "Happy Birthday." I wonder what that was like for my parents—to sing a song of celebration to someone who can't even smile, someone with lifeless eyes and a future that looks grim. Maybe they sang it with hope, trusting in God to care for their daughter when they couldn't.

Despite the sedation, my true self was deep down in that shell of a girl on life support. "I want cake," I wrote with a pen on paper. Simple and straightforward. I was like a little girl begging her mom for a slice of birthday cake. I missed tasting food, but for days, I had been what they call "NPO," which is short for the Latin phrase *nil per os*, meaning, nothing by mouth. Obviously, I couldn't eat while on a ventilator, but they hadn't even put a feeding tube in yet.

My numbers began moving in the right direction, though. I did something few people on life support get the chance to do. My father-in-law, Tim, had worked in the ICU before and he knew how important mobility was for someone on a ventilator. He spoke to my nurse, Paige, about it, suggesting they try to get me up and moving. The nurse said she would have the doctor call the physical therapy team. But it was late in the day on a Friday. That team doesn't work on the weekends, and they never made it up to my room.

"Would you want to try to get her up?" Paige asked him, knowing he was a physical therapist at a different hospital.

"Absolutely!" Tim said, eager to be able to practically help me in a time where everyone felt so helpless.

"I'll monitor the whole time and make sure all her tubes and cords don't get in the way," Paige said.

They asked me if I was up for trying to stand up. I didn't fully understand, but I hesitantly agreed, feeling the nervous, eager energy in the room. They slowly helped me sit up as the blue tube dangled from my mouth. Tim helped me move my legs to the side of the bed. I was fully sitting up for the first time in days. I held onto Tim's arms as he helped pull me up into a standing position. That's when I saw drops falling onto his brown shoes. It took a second, but then I realized those drops were coming from me. I could see the drool slowly falling from my mouth, a mouth I couldn't close if I wanted to. It was being held open for the tube to enter, tape clung to each of my cheeks.

That's drool? Why am I drooling? Globs of drool slowly dropped onto his shoes. He was laughing. *What's funny about this? Why can't I make myself stop?* I was grateful to be doing this with someone I knew and trusted, but I felt embarrassed to be drooling and unable to control it. He helped me take a step forward. Paige kept an eye on my vitals. Slowly, I took a step backward. Everyone in the room seemed to be holding their breaths. But my vitals remained stable, even improving a little. Tim was smiling, joking about the drool and thankful I was up and moving. Everyone was excited. This was big.

But all I felt was confusion. I don't think I even knew or understood that I was on a ventilator. I had no idea what a huge step that was. It is monumental to stand up while on life support. I've now learned in my research that the less sedation used while on a ventilator and the more the patient can be moving, the faster and easier their recovery is.

I also wasn't restrained. Many people on ventilators end up with their arms tied down because they don't understand what's going on. Naturally, they try to pull the tube out to take away the pain. But I'm a rule-follower. My arms were free. I'm afraid being restrained would have been even more scary and confusing. Plus, having my hands free meant I had the opportunity to try to communicate with my family when I wasn't fully sedated by using sign language or a paper and pen.

Everyone—myself included—wanted to see if I could come off life support. But it required a breathing test. The nurses would remove all my sedation and I'd be required to breathe for thirty minutes on my own. The ventilator was turned off, but the tube was still down my throat. If it all went well–my breathing rate was good and my heart rate didn't spike–I could come off the ventilator.

As they began to take me off all sedation, I wrote on my paper, "What in the world is going on? I'm so confused." Everyone tried their best to explain to me the situation. Soon the breathing test began and my heart rate spiked. I wasn't taking deep enough breaths, and I failed the test. My face fell in discouragement as I realized I was not coming off the ventilator. They turned the machine back on, filling my lungs with the air they needed. But I felt even further from relief.

They finally put a feeding tube in, but it didn't matter because surgery was still on the table. If I needed to go under again, my stomach had to be empty. I hadn't had food in five days. Because of this new tube, I couldn't stop gagging. So the nurses increased my sedation again to relieve me of the discomfort, and back to the darkness I went.

The next morning, things were starting to look up. My fever broke, and my white blood cell count was in the normal range for the first time. My condition was improving!

Except for one problem. My hemoglobin level had dropped. After a nurse changed my bedsheets, we quickly found out why. Remember how I had stopped breastfeeding leading up to my second hospital stay? Well, it turns out my body decided it was time to get my first period back since becoming pregnant with Ruthi. Can you even believe that? If you're a mama who's gotten her first postpartum period, you know they can be a real doozy. Now I had period cramps, wild hormones, abdomen pain from the infection, and two giant tubes down my throat without any sedation. But I was ready to do anything to get myself off that vent. Bring on round two of the breathing test.

When you are on a ventilator, you need to be suctioned out. With a tube down your throat, you can't swallow so the saliva runs down your trachea instead of being swallowed into your esophagus as usual. The fluid, as well as other secretions, can make it harder to breathe or even cause a respiratory infection. To prevent this, nurses suction all the fluid in your trachea using a suction catheter. It lasts for less than ten seconds, and it's not painful. The nurses had been suctioning me out multiple times a day, and I always felt I could breathe a little better afterward.

I wanted the best chance of getting off the ventilator, so I used my pen and paper to scribble a note to the nurses. "Can you suction me one last time or will that be worse?"

What I thought was a great idea quickly turned on me. I didn't realize that every time I had been suctioned out, I had also been sedated. I *fully* experienced being suctioned out for the first time, and I immediately regretted it. The feeling and sound of it mixed together was horrifying. That moment would come back to haunt me. I didn't have time to process it though, because I now needed to focus on breathing. Breathing on my own. Staying relaxed—as relaxed as you can be with a big tube down your throat.

Uncomfortable is the word that comes to mind, but it doesn't do being on a ventilator justice. It's a whole lot worse than being uncomfortable. It's disturbing to be fully aware of a tube that goes from your mouth down into your lungs. My throat burned and I could feel the tube deep into my chest. To not be able to speak or swallow or even close your mouth is distressing.

A nurse positioned my hospital bed into a sitting position to make it easier to breathe, then left the room. The clock ticked overhead. Thirty minutes. All I needed to do was to breathe for thirty minutes. Something so simple a few days ago now felt like life or death.

Travis sat next to me the whole time. My husband and I have been through dark places in our years together. We have endured much and somehow managed to survive it all—still together. I imagine watching me suffer through this medical trauma was the darkest place he's been.

At some point in my hospital stay, someone snapped a photo of him lying next to me in my hospital bed, his arm draped around me, as he slept. I can see the complete exhaustion in his body, but also in his mind and especially his heart. Yet, he can only sleep with an arm around me—protecting me, holding me close, knowing I'm still there, still breathing.

Travis played worship music for me during the breathing test. The song "The More I Seek You" by Kari Jobe softly played through the phone speaker. I motioned for Travis to put it on repeat. We listened to that song over and over. She talks about sitting at the feet of God and drinking from the cup in His hand. My favorites line says,

> *Lay back against you and breathe*
> *Feel your heartbeat.*[1]

---

1   Klaus, and Jobe, Kari, "The More I Seek You," Healing Waters, Pure Worship, 2005, 8

I pictured myself small, curled up in the palms of God's strong hands. The ventilator hurt, and I wished I could use my teeth to pull it out. It reminded me of when a dentist puts one of those devices in your mouth when you get X-rays. The way it pokes you and makes you want to gag. I was able to move the tube a little somehow by moving my teeth, but I felt so worried that I was cheating. Would they let me pass even though I had moved it around a little? Have I mentioned I'm a rule-follower?

At the same time, I knew I wouldn't pass the test with it jabbing me in the throat the whole time. I tried to close my eyes, and when I did, I felt like I was spinning. I would spin around and around, trying to focus on the song. I tried staying calm while the squares on the ceiling spun in circles and I focused on taking deep breaths. Over and over, I saw myself curled up safe and at peace in God's hands.

After thirty minutes, Dr. Ali came in and looked at all the monitors.

"Hmm," he said with concentration. "You're in the gray area. I'm not sure you're ready to come off yet."

I took a deep breath, steadying the spinning and my frustration.

"I'll need to see you go a little longer, Tiffany," he said, looking down at me.

"I cannot do this much longer," I scribbled on my paper. Yet, I felt determined to not let the last thirty minutes be for nothing. I wanted off this machine. And I wanted off it today.

"O K," I wrote in big letters, nodding my head slightly as I looked Dr. Ali in the eyes. I closed my eyes and continued to spin for another thirty minutes. Breathe in. Breathe out. Spin. Spin. *Lay back against You and breathe. Feel Your heartbeat.* Spin. Spin. Breathe in. Breathe out.

Sixty hours after being rocked by God that night in the ICU bed, I passed the breathing test. I had finally improved enough to come off the ventilator. My infectious disease doctor found the right mix of antibiotics to begin treating the infection, which lowered my pain levels enough so that I could breathe on my own. "I'm scared about how bad it will hurt coming out," I wrote on the paper before they removed the ventilator. "And also I don't want to be reintubated." I circled that last sentence. Travis says I gagged through the whole process, but I surprisingly don't remember it at all.

All that mattered was the tubes down my throat were removed! It was two days after my birthday, but what a gift it was. Breathing on my own was better than any birthday cake I had ever tasted.

CHAPTER 4

Blankets

Even though I walk through the darkest valley,
I will fear no evil, for You are with me; Your rod
and Your staff, they comfort me.

Psalm 23:4

"Hi, I'm Paige, and I'm your nurse," is what I expected her to say to me. Once I came off the ventilator, I met my nurse. I thought I was meeting her for the first time, so I waited for her to introduce herself. But it turns out she had been my nurse for days. I don't think she realized that I had no idea who she was. Paige had reddish brown hair up in a messy bun at the back of her head, blue scrubs, and glasses. My whole family knew Paige well and loved her by now. But all I knew was she was brushing my hair—without permission. I don't ever brush my hair when it's dry because my blond hair is naturally curly. It had taken years to learn how to care for my curls, and they were one of my favorite parts of myself. I had been awarded "best hair" in my senior yearbook.

I felt angry and confused that Paige—this woman I didn't

know—was brushing my hair into what felt like a lion's mane. I wrote on my paper: "Who told the nurse she could brush my hair?"

Travis chuckled but reassured me it was fine. He was too happy that I was off the ventilator to fully understand how confused I was, and I was too confused to realize this woman had been washing and brushing my hair for days.

What I felt, though, was more than confusion. Where I thought I would feel relief, darkness descended instead. A blanket of depression wrapped around me. I felt small and lost. Lots of family members in the waiting room wanted to come see me, but I suddenly felt like I was about to be paraded in front of them, like some kind of side show.

They were so happy I was off the ventilator, but I felt anything but happy. *Why? Are the girls here? I don't want the girls to see me like this. What do I even look like? I can't even talk yet. I'm not ready to see my babies. How can I be a mom right now?* I was so relieved when Travis told me the girls were not at the hospital. At the same time, I felt guilty for feeling that way. *Shouldn't I be desperate to see my babies?*

The number of emotions I felt was endless: grief, confusion, guilt, relief, sorrow, fear. I asked that the family come to see me in small groups and that they wouldn't stay long, writing it on my paper. They probably all figured I was exhausted. Physically I was, but even more so mentally and emotionally. It was that weighted blanket of depression that made me want to be alone, and yet at the same time I felt so lonely.

One or two at a time, they came into my room with smiles. I don't remember anything they said. It's not as if we could have a conversation. You can't speak after being intubated. I actually don't even remember who all was there, but one by one or two by two they left to go back to their homes or my home for the night.

The next day, I coughed a lot as my lungs worked to expel all the secretions. Paige gave me a small plastic suction catheter that sat on my hospital bed. It looked like the tool the dental hygienist uses to rinse out your mouth. As I would cough, I would grab this tool and stick it into my mouth, pressing the button to make it suction the mucus. This is called oral suctioning and helps keep your airways open. The tool allowed me to get rid of the secretions without having to spit constantly or swallow the mucus back down.

My voice gradually came back as a whisper by the next day, as my vocal cords began to recover. I could drink liquids, but it felt too new and difficult. I continued with ice chips until I tried small sips of water. But I was too scared to drink broth or anything else they offered me. After a coughing fit and suctioning my mouth out with my silver tool, I motioned for my mom to lean down close so she could hear me.

"I feel like . . . I'm fighting demons," I slowly whispered to her in my raspy and frail voice.

She nodded, patted my hand, and squeezed it. I know she was praying for me at that very moment, praying that God would fight the battle for me.

I spent another day in the ICU with round-the-clock care making sure I could fully breathe on my own and that I was continuing to improve. Now that I wasn't sedated, I could fully take in my surroundings. The room had one blue wall and a large bathroom inside the room. My visitors usually sat on the right side of my hospital bed, but there was one cream colored chair to my left. The left wall was all windows overlooking the hallway and nurses' station. That wall of windows had a glass door, and huge green curtains covered the whole wall for privacy.

Flowers and birthday balloons filled my room. There were photos framed of me with my girls sitting on a table directly in front of my bed. People had brought little mementos from my house or bought me little encouraging trinkets to place around my room. But despite all those gifts, I didn't feel much comfort in the sterile ICU room—not until I asked my mom to bring me the creamy white blanket from our couch at home, like a toddler longing for her beloved blankie.

It was my favorite throw blanket at Travis's parents' house when I would visit while we were dating. For our wedding, we ended up being gifted two of them. I loved cuddling on the couch with it, combing my fingers through its soft and slightly heavy texture.

On the nights my mom didn't sleep in the waiting room of the hospital, she stayed at our house, sleeping in our guest room. By 4 a.m. every morning, she'd be back at the hospital ready to keep watch over me. That morning, she brought the blanket. As soon as I touched the smooth fabric in my hands and felt the weight of it over my legs, I began to cry. Comfort washed over me in that moment, and I was stunned at how good something familiar felt, like a weight had been lifted from my chest.

Eight days after coming to the hospital, I was moved to a regular hospital room and out of the ICU. But I didn't feel relief. I felt fear. It was happening too soon. Dr. Ali's voice saying, "You'll have the best care in the ICU" rang in my head. I wanted the best care. I *needed* it. But I didn't get a choice or say in the matter.

Once I was settled in my new room, I asked my mom to bring me my Bible from my house, and she had it there for me early the next morning. I found myself in Jeremiah and took comfort in certain Scriptures. I took pictures of them and read them over and over, laying in my hospital bed.

> *Heal me, Lord, and I will be healed; save me and I will be saved, for you are the one I praise.*
>
> Jeremiah 17:14

> *But I will restore you to health and heal your wounds, declares the Lord...*
>
> Jeremiah 30:17

> *But I will rescue you on that day, declares the Lord; you will not be given into the hands of those you fear. I will save you; you will not fall by the sword but will escape with your life, because you trust in me, declares the Lord.*
>
> Jeremiah 39:17-18

The Scriptures gave me hope. I enjoyed having visitors and

was usually surprised at who showed up. One of my favorite people to visit me was Tressella. She came often, but what made her visits stand out to me the most was how she prayed for me. She didn't only tell me she *would* pray for me. She also asked what she could specifically pray for that day, and she laid hands on me and prayed over me right there. She and her husband were huge blessings to us during our suffering.

My sister-in-law Casey came to visit and brought me a pint of my favorite ice cream—Graeter's Black Raspberry Chip. I only took about two bites, and that's how everyone knew I wasn't feeling better yet. Normally, I could down that whole pint by myself. But my appetite wasn't back.

Being in a regular hospital room meant I was supposed to be recovering, but I still felt lots of pain. I had tests every day, doctors were in and out of my room, and the blanket of depression dragged me down. I couldn't help but wonder when the actual recovery would begin.

CHAPTER 5

Construction

For there is a proper time and procedure for
every matter, though a person may be weighed
down by misery.

Ecclesiastes 8:6

The truth about a road to recovery is that it's actually a one-lane
road full of backed-up traffic, bumper to bumper, with orange
cones lining the sides and tons of signs reminding you to drive
slowly or you'll get a fine. In other words, it's a construction zone.

Construction is a total pain. We've all been in it—stuck in
traffic, frustrated and impatient. Rather than call this my road to
recovery, I'd call it a construction zone because after every unexpected medical detour blocking me, I felt stuck, frustrated, and
impatient.

It was during this construction zone that I saw her face again:
my Hospital Angel. I was told I had fluid in my lungs, and it would
need to be extracted—my first detour. I had no idea what this
would entail or if it would hurt. I knew a needle would be involved,

and that was all I needed to know to be terrified. I was wheeled to a room where they would do the extraction.

In walked my Hospital Angel. Her face lit up! She talked as if she knew me and was so thankful I had survived. But I had no idea who she was. I didn't recognize her. Thanks to the sedation, there were many people I didn't remember.

She was with another woman who had tattoos on her arms. I told them how scared I was as I sat on the table. I asked the woman with the tattoos to talk to me the whole time. I stared at her tattoos trying to steady my shaking hands, while she told me about her kids and asked me about mine.

Meanwhile, my Hospital Angel stood behind me with my hospital gown open. She was doing an ultrasound on my back to see the fluid before inserting the needle.

"Tiffany," she said with surprise in her tone, "there's no fluid."

"What?" I replied in confusion, my fists still clenched in fear.

"There's no fluid there," she confirmed as she began to put the ultrasound machine away. "We don't have to do the procedure."

I smiled as wide as I could as I was wheeled back on my hospital bed to my room. My family couldn't believe it, and we chalked it up to another miracle. It was when I was back in my room that the memory hit me like a cool breeze to the face.

"She was the one who listened to me," I said out of nowhere as it all came back to me. "She was from the IR team, the one who ordered the X-ray."

"The girl who couldn't find the fluid?" asked my mom in a chair across from my hospital bed.

"Yes, she saved me that day," I said. "That's why she recognized me. I didn't realize who she was!"

That's when we began calling her my Hospital Angel. I would see her twice more, running into her randomly throughout the hospital, and each time she would do whatever she could to check on me, care for me. Once, she came across me lying in my hospital bed in the transport hallway, waiting for someone to wheel me back to my room. She spotted me and stopped to see how I was.

"Tiffany! How are you feeling?" she asked.

"Better. I've been having a lot of pain," I said, pointing to my side. "So I just had an ultrasound on my liver. They are worried something's wrong with it." I paused.

"Listen, I wanted to tell you that I didn't realize who you were last time," I suddenly said, looking up into her brown eyes. She stood next to the bed, nodding in understanding. "I didn't remember you because the sedation made me forget a lot of things. But I remembered later. I just wanted you to know that I feel like you saved me."

She smiled, never breaking eye contact, content with listening despite whatever she needed to get done.

"I just wanted to thank you," I said.

"It was the perfect teaching example," she replied. "I was able to teach the student who was with me that day that we don't just care about the drain. We are there to check on the whole patient. I'm so glad to see you are doing better."

My transporter arrived so she wished me well as he began to push my bed out of the hallway. As I was being wheeled into the elevator, my Hospital Angel came running around the corner.

"Tiffany, I checked with the tech," she said, rushing to tell me the news. "Your liver is fine!"

"Thank you!" I yelled out as the elevator doors closed. I didn't need to worry about my liver anymore. The truth was I didn't need to worry at all. My Hospital Angel was one of the many ways God was taking care of me. That liver ultrasound was a detour on my road to recovery but now I was back on track.

That same day, my nurse, Bailey, with her wavy dark hair and big blue eyes, removed the central line from my neck. A central line is a thin, flexible tube inserted into the large vein near your heart. They use this method rather than an IV when someone is intubated because it can be used for much longer. It allows them to deliver medicine and fluids, and draw blood samples quickly and easily, right from the patient's neck.

When Bailey removed mine, it felt like ripping off a Band-

Aid times one hundred, probably because there had been a lot of adhesive around it to keep it in place. Without my central line, I would need a regular IV in my elbow. But my veins never cooperate, and because Bailey felt sympathy for how much I had been through in the past week, she chose not to keep sticking me until I bruised. She called in an ultrasound tech to come to my room and use an ultrasound machine to find the vein and put my IV in. It was so much easier, and I wished that I could always have an ultrasound tech anytime I needed an IV or a blood draw.

Bailey also taught me a trick for my daily shots in my belly. Every day, a nurse would give me a shot to keep me from getting blood clots. Bailey showed me how she would pinch the skin before injecting me and told me to ask any other nurses to do the same. The pinching helped it hurt less, but those shots stung like some kind of fire hornet you'd read about in a fantasy novel.

I had been afraid that the central line in my neck would scare my two-year-old. So once it was removed, I Facetimed with Raylee for the first time. A big smile swept across my face as I saw my little girl again, but it was hard to keep my toddler's attention. As she bounced across the phone screen, I wished I could reach through and pull her close, smell her soft hair, and rub her back.

"We have missed you Raylee Bear!" I said. "Are you having fun?"

Several toddlers crowded around the camera, all talking at once. Raylee showed us the toy she was playing with as Cara tried to corral the others away. It felt good to see her smile and check in on Ruthi too, but it also made my heart heavy. When would I see them again without a screen separating us?

I was constantly undergoing tests to check on my condition and infection. At one point, my hemoglobin dropped again, and they discussed a blood transfusion. But the issue was that a transfusion lowers your immune system, and I desperately needed mine to fight off my infection. We thought it was about to be another detour, but this time the construction zone was clear—I never ended up needing that transfusion.

Two days after leaving the ICU, I was significantly improving so I expected to be discharged soon. I was doing notably well with physical therapy, and I was eating again. But as I began to recover, I also felt restless, trapped, powerless. The hospital felt like a prison. I confessed to Travis one day how down I felt.

"You can walk across the street if you wanted to," I said in a whisper as he lay next to me in my hospital bed. "I can't even leave this room."

A little later, Travis said he needed to check on something. He came back with a wheelchair. He had asked at the nurse's station if he could use one and take me for a ride around the hospital. They agreed. I think they had gotten to know Travis. A lot of times he took care of little issues that normally a nurse would handle. He had learned where supplies were and would get them himself rather than asking a nurse. Even though he probably wasn't supposed to, I think they appreciated his help.

One of the nurses told Travis about an outdoor garden area on one of the floors. He helped me into my new ride, wrapped my favorite blanket around me, and off we went. For the first time in weeks, the widest smile splashed across my face. I took a selfie in my wheelchair with a pillow propped behind me, my hair pulled back with a blue headband on. Travis stood behind me in his old gray Purdue hoodie next to my IV stand, his beard a little unruly since he hadn't been worried about his own hygiene in quite some time.

On one of the floors, we came close to the entrance doors. Around the corner walked my parents and Aunt Traci.

"Oh my gosh! Look at you!" my mom said, whipping out her phone to take a photo of me, finally out of my room.

"Well, we sure didn't expect to see you around the corner," my dad said.

Aunt Traci beamed at me, and I grinned right back. My mom leaned down for a gentle side hug and then took another picture. As a mom myself I can imagine the joy she felt in seeing me smile—finally some life in my eyes.

Travis took me to the floor with the outdoor garden. The January temps iced our bones and only cement walls, no greenery, welcomed us—but it was glorious. I loved breathing in the fresh air versus the stale hospital musk while the freezing cold brushed my cheeks. It felt like waking up in the morning with something exciting planned for the day. My blue hospital booties peaked out underneath my creamy white blanket draped from my shoulders down to my feet.

Travis rolled me back to the hospital room with a small but mighty dose of hope. I needed that small taste of freedom because what the surgeon said to me the next day felt like a punch to my abdomen. An abdomen that was in recovery no less.

CHAPTER 6

Detours

The people walking in darkness have seen a
great light; on those living in the land of deep
darkness a light has dawned.

Isaiah 9:2

"Your CT results came back," my surgeon said, not looking into my
eyes. He never made eye contact. "You have developed another
abscess right on top of your bladder. We will need to put another
drain in."

I nodded, trying hard to keep my lip from quivering. I held in
the tears as best I could. I didn't want to break down in front of this
man who wouldn't even look me directly in the eye. He and my
hospitalist had been so optimistic the day before. They acted as if
I'd be going home soon. They thought this CT scan would come
back clear, and if it did, they would discharge me.

The surgeon left the room quickly, as he always did, like he
didn't have time for me. Perhaps he felt guilty for dismissing my
signs of sepsis, but he could have at least shown me empathy.

As soon as the door shut behind him, I asked to go to the bathroom. Travis helped me up and walked me in. The door closed behind us, leaving my mom and Aunt Traci on the other side, and I broke down. Massive sobs erupted from my chest as the disappointment and fear of never getting to leave spilled out of me onto the hard bathroom floor.

But it was more than that. He said I had to have another drain put in. I'd had a drain already and all I could think about was how it went the last time. My body went septic. *What if it reacted that way again? What if I had to go back on the ventilator?*

The blanket of depression felt so heavy that evening that I began googling "depression after ICU" or "wanting to die after ventilator" in hopes of getting some kind of answer. *What was wrong with me? Why couldn't I sleep? Why was I scared to fall asleep?* Google told me that PTSD was normal after being in the ICU. That gave me some comfort in validating the huge waves of emotions that felt like they were knocking me over and over, like I was unable to stand up and catch my breath.

It wasn't until a year later that I learned what Post Sepsis Syndrome (PSS) and Post Intensive Care Syndrome (PICS) are. I wish a nurse, a doctor, the chaplain, or the therapist I saw while in the hospital had told me about these conditions so I would have known that everything I was experiencing was normal, so I would have known what to expect as I recovered. But either none of them knew, or none of them took the time to make sure I knew that mental health issues are a part of medical trauma.

PSS is a condition that can cause short or long-term physical, medical, cognitive, and psychological issues after recovering from sepsis. The problems may not even become apparent until several weeks after you come home from the hospital. This condition affects up to half of sepsis survivors.

PICS is common among ICU patients who were sedated and/or placed on a ventilator. These survivors can have cognitive problems a year after discharge. PICS often results in fear, anxiety, depression, hallucinations, and even delirium. Thankfully, I never experienced hallucinations or delirium, but I've heard stories from people who have. Most of them had their arms restrained while on the ventilator and thought the nurses were trying to kill them.

I would experience hair loss—which is a result of all the trauma—insomnia, and brain fog. I couldn't think of the right word or I'd mix up words. I experienced poor appetite and memory loss. I'd also have nightmares, flashbacks of being suctioned out, anxiety, depression, suicidal thoughts, fatigue, panic attacks, and mood swings in the months to come.

I opened up with Travis that nights were the hardest for me. The tests were done, the visitors gone, and I knew I wouldn't be able to sleep well. I dreaded nighttime. The blanket of depression felt its heaviest in the darkness. That night, Travis had the bright idea to pull his couch-turned-bed as close as it could be to my hospital bed. He lowered my guardrail and laid next to me, covering us in one large blanket.

"I'll stay awake for as long as you need," he whispered to me. "You can talk to me or we can just lay here."

The next day was a a detour I was dreading—January 31. The day my second drain would be put in. I had now been in the hospital for eleven days. The chaplain waited with me in the transport hallway before the procedure. After a few visits with me, she understood how scared I was and didn't want me to be alone as I waited.

When the doctor came into the transport hallway to meet me, I asked him to explain what would happen. Yes, I'd had a drain put in only a week before, but I had no memory of the procedure.

He explained I would have anesthesia and would be asleep for the whole thing. I was finally able to take a full breath knowing this, and although I was still scared, I had no choice but to lay there as they wheeled my bed into the procedure room.

Nurses were busy washing my skin and laying a big blue drape over me while I lay there crying. I wanted them to just put me out so I could calm down. Eventually, I drifted off into blackness as the tears dribbled off the sides of my face.

Thankfully, this drain gave me no complications. It was much smaller than my first one, round and hung off the right side of my abdomen. They drained 30 milliliters, or about two tablespoons, of fluid from my abscess as soon as it was in place.

I graduated from physical therapy that day too. I find this to be yet another miracle. I was supposed to go to rehab or at least do at-home physical therapy, but I had made enough progress walking the hall outside of my hospital room to graduate.

But even with all that progress, I felt discouraged. I watched a nurse write on the big white board "Feb 1." I had told myself I would be home before February showed up. Instead, I lay there staring at the same walls, the same small TV in the upper left corner, the same window I could barely see out of. *When would I ever recover? When would I get out of here?*

The answer came quickly.

"I'm ready to discharge you," my surgeon said standing in my doorway.

I looked at him in surprise. "Really?"

He nodded in his impersonal, stoic way. But I didn't care. I was going home. I was going to see my babies again!

Part of the discharge, though, meant I had to walk down the hallway. Just like with my breathing test, I was weak but determined. I pulled on my gripper socks and rotated out of the bed. With a deep breath, I took one step. Then another and another. Three hundred feet down the hall, I knew I was ready.

Instead of at-home IV antibiotics, my infectious disease doctor allowed me to switch to oral antibiotics. This had been a hindrance in coming home. We couldn't find an at-home transfusion clinic that took our insurance. It was a bump in the road that had finally smoothed out. I breathed in relief. Now I wouldn't have to chase a toddler and baby with an IV stuck in my arm. That doctor signed off on being discharged too. I was going home!

It felt surreal as we pulled into the driveway of our home for the first time in two weeks. That first day, we decided to let me get acclimated back to our home and rest as much as possible before our girls arrived. I slept most of the day. What a difference it made to sleep in a real bed without anyone waking me to draw my blood.

The next day, I sat in the gray glider in the corner of our living room as Raylee came barreling into the house. She hugged Travis as he picked her up and whirled her around.

"Mommy was very sick, but now she's getting better," Travis explained as he set Raylee down next to me. "So we have to be really gentle with her."

I couldn't pick Raylee up the way her dad could, but she could climb onto my lap for hugs or sit next to me as I read her books. That first day with our girls home wasn't quite as wonderful as I had imagined because I had a terrible headache. After getting hugs and seeing them for a little bit, I went back to our bedroom for a long nap.

That's what most of those first days looked like. The girls were cared for by their dad and grandma while I sat and watched and tried to participate as much as I could, spending every afternoon sleeping as my body healed.

Some of the orange cones of my recovery construction zone had been removed, but it was far from over. Construction always tends to take longer than expected, doesn't it? At my first follow-up appointment after being home for a few days, the surgeon broke the news.

"This isn't something that is going to be over in a week or two," he admitted, looking down on me as I lay on the table. He had removed the small round drain that had been attached to me. "It will be months before you feel like yourself again."

I bawled during the drive home as I looked out at the drivers next to our car. Their lives were going on as normal, and it felt like mine had stopped. I was ready for my light to turn green, and yet I was only given a yellow. This was not what I was expecting, and especially not what I wanted. *When could I be strong enough to take care of my girls without needing a nap? We wanted three kids. Could we have more? Would this affect the rest of my life?*

PART 2

Surrender

CHAPTER 7

Earthquakes

God is our refuge and strength, an ever-present
help in trouble. Therefore we will not fear,
though the earth gives way and the mountains
fall into the heart of the sea, though its waters
roar and foam and the mountains quake with
their surging.

Psalm 46:1-3

It was a hot and humid summer, just five months after I had been released from the hospital. I was physically recovered for the most part and was working through the mental effects of my trauma. They had recently been triggered when a friend named Laura back in my hometown had died unexpectedly that month. She collapsed in her home and was flown to a hospital. Everyone prayed, but she didn't make it.

"I prayed that God would heal her the way he healed you," a mutual friend wrote me online as she told me what happened. She meant it with the best intentions. She was grateful for my healing and wanted the same for our friend, just as I did. But that comment felt like a punch in the stomach. It was the first time I felt survivor's guilt. The questions immediately began pouring into my mind. *Why didn't she survive like I did? Why was I healed but others aren't? Why am I still alive? Why me?*

It was not the last time I would ask these questions. Countless people I knew would die over the next several years, many of whom were young mothers like I was, and every time I would feel that ache. That could have been me. Why did they die? Why did He heal me?

I think of the man in Jerusalem from John 5 who sat by the pool of Bethesda, paralyzed and waiting for healing for thirty-eight years. He sat by that pool every day for years, surely knowing the other people sitting there too. Perhaps they bonded in their illnesses and disabilities. And Jesus came and healed this one man, but none of the others. His immediate reaction, I'm sure, was shock and joy. But later, did he have thoughts of survivor's guilt? Did he question, "Why me and not them?"

As he learned of the death of others who used to sit by the pool with him, did the survivor's guilt feel like a heavy weight on his chest? I know that heavy weight. What about the others sitting at the pool, watching that man get healed while they sat still unable to curl their toes? They were also waiting for healing. Did they begin to question, "Why not me?"

Haven't we all asked this when our prayers go unanswered? I know the heartbreak of loss. I know the questions that come with it. I know how unfair it feels. I know it all too well. Because while He answered our prayers in that hospital in 2020, He didn't answer my prayers in another hospital.

Four years before my time in the ICU, I was in an emergency room in Muncie, Indiana. Travis and I were moving to Missouri, so we had stopped to stay with his parents and tell everyone goodbye before we took the trip west. We had only been married for two years, and this was our third place to live—six hours away from all our families.

The whole family had come over for dinner and we had

planned to tell everyone that we were expecting our first baby. But as everyone arrived for the dinner, I began to bleed. The announcement never happened. We finally went to the ER after I had been bleeding for a couple hours, unsure of what exactly we were supposed to do.

As I lay in the hospital bed while they examined me, I saw more blood than I had ever seen. The doctor confirmed what I already knew: we had lost the baby. Miscarriage was suddenly added to my regular vocabulary. The nurses gave me morphine to help with my pain, which was when I discovered my adverse reaction to it. It put me into what I can only describe as a coma. This was the first moment I experienced medical trauma.

When we were leaving the ER that night in Indiana, we were told to make a doctor's appointment right away in our new town to make sure everything had been expelled. A few days later, we moved into our hotel in Missouri while we looked for houses to live in. Then we went to the new hospital on the military base. When I told the receptionist the appointment was for a miscarriage, sympathy swept across her face. She quickly got a nurse's attention, and they took us to a separate room to wait alone instead of next to women with round bellies and expectant dreams.

We met our nurse, Alicia, that day. With her sandy blond hair pulled back to reveal her sweet round face, her soft-spoken and kind nature told me I wasn't alone in this loss. She got us set up and ready for the doctor to do a vaginal ultrasound. When the screen next to the doctor's table came to life, we all saw it: a small circle inside my uterus. There was something there, though: movement. Something was pulsing visibly on that large screen.

Hope leaped into my heart. I began silently mouthing, "Please save my baby. Please Lord, give us a miracle. Save my baby. Please." My mind repeated the prayer as the doctor went to get a second opinion, not sure what he was seeing. He didn't want us to get our hopes up, but I could see the hope in his own eyes. He was an older man with gray hair and wrinkled skin. How many lost babies had he seen? How many times had he seen miracles? *Please give us a miracle, God. Please save my baby.*

"It looks like a gestational sac, but I can't be sure," he said. "You see the fluttering?"

We nodded. Yes, we definitely saw it. That's what a heartbeat should look like, right? *Please save my baby. Please God.*

"It could be a baby's heartbeat, but it could also just be your heartbeat," he said, still unsure.

The second doctor refused to give us an answer, as he couldn't confirm either way. But unlike the first doctor, he didn't have hope in his eyes. It felt as if this second doctor had seen one too many losses. He tried to prepare me that most likely it was either my heartbeat or leftover tissue pulsing on the screen. *Lord, save my baby. What a beautiful story this will be. What a miracle!*

After the second doctor left the room, the hope-filled doctor said it could have been that I had twins and we lost the first, but the second was still there. He couldn't be sure, and he didn't want to rule one way or another. *Give us a miracle, Lord.* The only way to know for sure was to get blood work drawn to see if my HCG levels were rising or falling. He also ordered another ultrasound with a better machine.

That next morning, I had my fourth vaginal ultrasound in five days. I was weary from the physical aspect of it all, but even more so from the wondering whether I should rejoice in the life inside me or grieve its death. I stared at the ultrasound technician's face as she pushed buttons on her machine. She made no facial expressions, giving away no answers. I knew if the news were good, she would have told us. I knew if she was remaining stoic it must mean there was no miracle. Tears slowly spilled down my face.

"Did you see what they saw yesterday?" I asked, desperate for answers.

"Yes, kind of," she replied.

"Is it—"

"No," she interrupted. "I'm sorry."

I couldn't help myself. I couldn't hold it in. I couldn't wait to be alone in the room with Travis or even to be fully clothed. The sorrow and grief erupted out of me like a geyser, and at that moment I didn't care if the whole hospital heard my sobs.

I was rocked by God in that moment, but I don't mean it in the comforting sense. It was in losing our first baby that my faith was tested like never before. It rocked like an earthquake—shaken so hard you find out whether the foundation can hold. I didn't get the miracle I had prayed for. He didn't save my baby. Two hours later, while sitting in our car, we found out that Travis' grandma had died—an aftershock we weren't expecting, rocking us again before we had time to brace ourselves.

We signed papers for a house that day, waited as the movers emptied the truck full of our belongings into our new home, and then immediately left for the six-hour drive back to Indiana for her funeral—all while I continued to bleed. I looked up at the moon shining bright in the dark sky as we drove that night. All I could think about was how unfair it was that my baby wouldn't get a funeral.

I stood inside the funeral home during the visitation as someone trying to comfort me in our baby's loss said to me, "Everything happens for a reason."

I wanted to scream. It was at that moment that I vowed to never utter those words to someone ever again. I learned that day that reasons don't take away sorrow. Even if there were a reason, it wouldn't bring me comfort.

When my own grandparents walked into the funeral home, I melted into my grandma's arms as we both cried big tears. I didn't know they would be there. They had driven three hours to be there for us in our grief. Words aren't needed to comfort someone, many times your presence is enough.

Too many days and nights, I would sit inside the small shower of our new house in Missouri as the water poured over me, mixing with my tears. I would weep—sometimes screaming out if Travis was at work, but always at least screaming in my head: "Where were You? Didn't You hear me? Couldn't You see me laying there begging You to save my baby?"

I would cry until there were no tears left. I would question God like never before. *Are You really good?*

I have both received and been denied a miracle on a hospital bed. I have questioned and doubted. During the grief of that loss, I felt betrayed by God. It was the first time I felt like God had walked away from me. He felt so silent.

Only because of the foundation that had already been built was I able to survive this earthquake and keep pursuing God. It felt as if He had walked away, and I had to chase Him down. I don't believe God ever truly walks away from us, but at that time in my life it felt like it.

There are times when God is distant, but He's never actually absent. It's like when I am putting away laundry in one room while my children play on the floor next to me. When I walk out of the room, they can't see me and they feel like I am gone. But I am still there in the house, only in the next room over. I can still hear them and see them as I walk back and forth from the closet to the laundry basket. I'm giving them the chance to learn to play independently while I continue to watch over them and protect them. They doesn't realize it, but I'm working all around them. All children must learn and grow to trust that we haven't left them completely.

Curt Thompson speaks on this in his book, *Anatomy of the Soul*, when he says,

> *[God] was not absolutely absent but rather more distant. God's movement toward and away from us is one means by which He encourages growth in our flexibility and resilience in the face of the emotional distress we sense in His relative absence.*[1]

We can trust that God still hears us and can see us, like a mama in the next room who always comes back and never leaves her

---

1 Thompson, Curt, *Anatomy of the Soul: Surprising Connections between Neuroscience and Spiritual Practices that can Transform Your Life and Relationships*, (Carol Stream, Tyndale Refresh, 2010), 187.

baby alone. It felt like God was playing a cruel game with me when we lost that baby. But God wasn't playing hide-and-seek despite how it felt. I now recognize He is all around us, continuing His work—just like how we walk from room to room putting away the laundry to complete our chores and keep the house running.

I didn't understand this yet though, and I began wandering around, searching for God in all the rooms. I began pouring through my Bible and other Christian books, desperately trying to find the answers to all my questions. How is this even fair? Why would You let me get pregnant in the first place? You could have saved me from this suffering.

Unfortunately, in all my searching, there was no straightforward answer that took away the pain. And just like I learned at that funeral with those well-meaning but ignorant words—no reason would take away my grief. Even if I had all the answers and saw the intricacies of how this loss played into God's grand scheme of goodness, it wouldn't have taken away the sorrow of the loss. I had to live through the grief. Because we don't need to know His plan, we just need to know His presence.

I don't believe God took away my baby. I believe this fallen world did that all on its own. What we struggle to grapple with, though, is that God allowed it. He didn't answer my prayer or give me the miracle. I truly believe, despite how distant I felt from God in those months, that He was weeping with me. He was present. Jesus grieved with me just as he grieved with Mary and Martha when their brother, Lazarus, died. In John 11, we see that Jesus would go on to raise Lazarus from the dead. He knew he was about to bring Lazarus back to life—and yet, Jesus still wept from the loss. God knew He would bring good from my miscarriage, but it didn't stop Him from crying with me.

Despite the broken and tragic world with all of its heartbreak, He can bring good from even the worst of situations. Sometimes, however, we don't see the good—only He sees it, and that makes it even harder to trust. Hebrews 11:1 says, "Now faith is confidence in what we hope for and assurance about what we do not see."

There is nothing wrong with questioning God. He is big enough to handle all our questions. He's safe enough. In fact, He longs for us to come to Him.

We can look back at the first sin in the history of the world. It wasn't a sin that Eve questioned God. But it became a problem when she didn't take those questions to God. The serpent tempted her, and she began to question what God had said and if He had her best interest in mind. But instead of going to God—who walked through and visited her in the garden—with her feelings and doubts and questions, she dealt with them on her own. This caused her to turn to sin and eventually hide from God in her shame.

How would the future have been different if she had sought out God and asked, "What was it you said about that tree in the center of the garden? Can you explain to me why it is forbidden? Can you assure me that this is for my good because I'm honestly having some doubts here."

I picture God putting His arm around her and saying, "Let's go for a walk. I'd love to explain this to you more and help you trust in Me."

It's the same way I hope my own kids will feel safe enough to come to me with all their questions about the world around them, about who they are and who God is. I welcome it, the way God welcomes it from us.

God wants to wrap His arms around us when we are hurt or disappointed or doubting. He wants to kiss us on our foreheads and remind us we are safe with Him. He doesn't call us weak or ungrateful. There is no shame in bringing all our questions and hurts to the One who can fully heal and love us through them.

By coming to Him after an earthquake, He can repair any damages and strengthen our foundations. Sometimes that means getting into the Word of God or spending more time in prayer, while other times it may mean seeking therapy like I did. When we do the work after an earthquake to repair ourselves and heal from trauma, we strengthen our foundations, reinforcing ourselves for the next earthquake we encounter. Suffering inevitably can help us become more like Jesus. It deepens our roots if we let it, and it refines us into the people God has called us to be. Ultimately, it's not about whether we receive the healing or our prayers are left unanswered–what matters is who we become through the suffering.

When we bring our hurts to God, we grow our trust in Him. It is only in being vulnerable that we can practice trust. I am thankful that even within my pain, my foundation was sturdy enough that my faith did not crumble. Instead, it led me to pursue Him more. Eventually, I came to the realization that I had to proclaim my trust in God even in the doubts and questions.

One day I sat at my kitchen table with my Bible open, alone in our house while Travis was at work. I spoke out loud, "I trust you, God." It was not easy to say. My heart didn't feel like trusting. My heart felt cautious and unsure. But I began proclaiming my trust in God every day—in the shower, at my desk as I wrote blog posts, while making dinner, driving in my car. Lauren Daigle's song "Trust in You" became my anthem, and I listened to it on repeat. It talks about trusting God even when He doesn't answer our prayers.

I proclaimed my trust in God with my lips over and over until my heart finally caught up. I don't know why some prayers get answered and others don't or why some people get healed, and others die. If I knew the answer, this book would easily become a number one seller because that's something we all question.

I only know that I am merely a speck in all of creation. I can't see the ultimate plan. I can't even see the next step most of the time. But I have learned over and over the same main truths: God is sovereign. He will only allow what is for my good and His glory, and because of that I can trust Him.

Practicing trust is what I had to do over and over after my miscarriage, and it all started inside a CrossFit gym.

CHAPTER 8

Warrior

The weapons we fight with are not the
weapons of the world. On the contrary, they
have divine power to demolish strongholds.

2 Corinthians 10:4

Every January, the memories come rushing back. Each date brings
a "this is the day ____ happened." The week of my birthday always
holds the most conflicting feelings for me. It's the same week that
I experienced my first miscarriage, the one that rocked my faith
in a whole new way. Four years later, that same week, was when I
was moved to the ICU and almost died of sepsis.

But now—years after both those experiences—my birthday
reminds me that I am still here, still breathing. Neither of those
experiences, which felt as if they would kill me, actually did. I
survived. During that week, I am reminded that when I am weak
God is strong. That He heals my body and my heart. I am also
reminded that God still does miracles, and He will take care of my
children even if I can't. I can trust Him.

It is a time of both grief and gratitude. My body reminds me of the trauma I faced while Facebook memories pop up, reminding me of the hundreds of prayers that were lifted for me. I especially love reading the prayers that were written out right there on Facebook, as if they are being said for me in that exact moment years later.

I recall every year the number of people who showed up at the hospital to visit and support us. Our church family stepped up and made sure we had meals every night for months after I came home from the hospital.

My friends Elizabeth and Kelsie came to the hospital with big gift bags full of things like pajamas, headbands, ChapStick, notebooks—so many things I could use during my stay. The pajamas especially came in handy when I realized all my clothes I had worn when coming to the hospital had been cut off and discarded. I would have had nothing to wear when I was finally discharged if not for the soft gray pajamas they gave me. Along with that, we were given more gift cards and treats than I could count, even a whole set of birthday cake scented soaps and lotions!

The messages of love I received reminded me in the hardest, darkest times during recovery and beyond, that I was valued, and my life had purpose. My friend Kariana sent a message I saved on my phone for keeping. It read, "I'm genuinely inspired and encouraged by you. I'm so grateful you're still with us on earth. I know this is our temporary home, but I'm so so so happy you're home with your babies."

People cared for me and my family in ways I will forever be grateful for, but still the grief doesn't disappear easily or completely. Every January I relearn that grief and gratitude, sorrow and joy, can co-exist. Often in life we must hold them both at the same time, which stretches us, the way the yoga pose downward dog pulls at our leg muscles.

After my miscarriage, a woman named Julie invited me to a Holy Yoga class. We knew each other so little. I didn't even call her a friend yet. I had never heard of such a class, and I'd never done any type of yoga before. But I decided to see what it was about, so I went out the night before and bought myself a cheap yoga mat. I figured if nothing else, maybe I could connect with Julie more. We had just moved to Missouri, and I didn't know anyone yet. I was also curious about Holy Yoga. What makes it holy? I felt disconnected from God and His voice, so this seemed like it was worth a shot.

The morning after buying my cheap yoga mat, I walked into a large garage converted into a CrossFit gym. Two of the garage doors were open, letting in a soft morning breeze. Weights and jump boxes, ropes and exercise balls all sat along the wall. As I walked in, Julie waved at me with a big smile, quickly introducing me to Jen the instructor. Jen pulled her hair back into a ponytail as she welcomed me to the class.

I fumbled into my purse to pull out the seven dollars to pay for the class and found a spot on the floor next to Julie to lay my mat. Two other women were behind us doing stretches on their own mats. Worship music softly played in the background as Jen got us started with prayer and then some basic stretches. She talked about focusing in on our breaths and extending our exhales. As we held a pigeon pose, Jen read us Scripture.

I breathed in and out and felt a peace wash over me. I came back the next week. Then the week after that. This Holy Yoga session became a big part of my learning to trust God again. It became my church every week, my chance to pause and listen for God. The class was small, and many mornings it was just Julie and me following along with Jen. A couple of times I was the only one in the class.

We would flow from pose to pose, and during a resting pose, Jen would read us a short lesson she had written or a devotional from a book. At the end of the class, we would lie in corpse pose, which is just laying stretched out on your back. Jen would walk over to me, anoint my forehead with oil, and give the back of my neck a short massage while she prayed over me. The lavender smell enveloped me as the words to the song playing swirled around the room. Many times, I found myself in tears.

In a time where I felt God had walked away, where I could no longer hear or feel Him near me, that yoga class gave me the chance to finally hear His quiet, gentle whispers to my heart. Jen's lesson, Scriptures, or the worship music in the background became a vessel for God's voice.

I could hear Him again. Could trust Him again. I learned that I could hold grief and gratitude at the same time, but that it stretches you, sometimes to your limits. Stretching creates tension. We are familiar with that tension in our physical bodies. But it is true for the stretching of our hearts as well—the tension of holding two sacred, yet conflicting, emotions at once. That tension can cause aches and pains. And yet, just like in yoga, stretching is crucial for restoration and healing.

That Holy Yoga class renewed my body after the physical exhaustion of miscarrying, but most of all, it restored my heart. The suffering I have experienced, specifically during the loss of our first baby, has always been a pain I have wrestled with God over. It may be a struggle I never understand.

The story of Jacob wrestling with God at the Jordan River comes to my mind. It's found in Genesis 32. Jacob continued to wrestle all night long until God dislocated his hip at daybreak. But Jacob still would not stop wrestling unless God agreed to bless him.

Verse 28 tells us God renamed Jacob, calling him "Israel" because he wrestled with God and "overcame." That morning, Jacob became an overcomer—a warrior—but he walked away with a limp.

I feel like Jacob who just won't stop wrestling, and yet God calls me an overcomer. At the same time, I limp. Because of the suffering I've endured, I struggle to trust God completely. That distrust, that doubt, is my limp—a limp I may have for the rest of my life. One day when I was really wrestling it out with God about why my baby died, He reminded me that no matter how much I wrestle Him, He will never beat me up. What a comfort it was to know he welcomed the wrestling and refused to hurt me during it.

Yoga flitted away from my life after that season of my miscarriage when we moved to a new state, but it always seems to return when my body needs it most. While recovering from sepsis, yoga was a workout I could handle to get my body back in shape. It focused on breathing, something I was still gaining strength in after fluid-filled lungs and four days on a ventilator.

I would turn on YouTube videos and follow along while Raylee crawled underneath me every time I arched into a downward dog. The instructor, Adriene, would tell us to stand in mountain pose and thank our body for what it could do. Instead, I stood there and thanked God for my body.

Doing those yoga sessions made me so thankful for my healing, the ability to even do yoga, for never needing rehab, or never having amputations. There is a pose called warrior that symbolizes our ability to overcome. Many times as I exercise, I think of myself as a warrior. Last year, Cara and I started working out regularly and keeping each other accountable. We decided to focus on planking and seeing how long we could hold a plank, pushing ourselves to go longer each time.

When I prop up my body with only my forearms and toes, I remind myself of the warrior I am—of what I have endured and overcome. But ultimately, I remember that it is not my strength that has helped me survive so much suffering. That I am completely weak. It is all within God's strength that I am still breathing and walking and holding a plank. Yet, He still calls me warrior. In 2 Corinthians 12:9-11, we read:

> But he said to me, "My grace is sufficient for you, for my power is made perfect in weakness." Therefore, I will boast all the more gladly about my weaknesses, so that Christ's power may rest on me. That is why, for Christ's sake, I delight in weaknesses, in insults, in hardships, in persecutions, in difficulties. For when I am weak, then I am strong.

He makes me an overcomer because I surrender to Him. We may be challenged and tested; we may suffer with physical and emotional pain. But God can take all the suffering and questions and doubts and use it to make us into secure and fearless warriors.

He builds our strength, our focus, our courage, and our confidence. We grow when we are stretched to our limits. We grow when we wrestle with Him. And that's when He makes us into warriors.

There was a time during Covid-19 when my anxiety crippled me. We had finally gone out into the world to visit my family, risking my immune system if Covid-19 was as dangerous as we had heard. My fears were overwhelming one day during that visit, and my trust in God was clouded by my own doubts. I took comfort knowing Job had wavered too. He says in chapter 23 that he couldn't see or find God. I've been there, Job.

But in verse 10, Job says, "When He has tested me, I will come forth as gold" (Job 23:10). Job knew that even though he couldn't see (or hear or feel) God, God would bring him through that trial as purified gold. There will be days when we will doubt. But each trial is purifying us like gold. It is forming self-discipline like doing yoga's tree pose over and over. There will be days where I stand shaky and fall over. But each time I stand up tall, I'm building that trust. And like tree pose, building trust takes practice.

CHAPTER 9

Send Me

They will have no fear of bad news; their
hearts are steadfast, trusting in the Lord.

Psalms 112:7

A month after my ICU stay, the whole world was going on lock-
down as the pandemic swept from country to country. Churches
weren't meeting, restaurants were drive-through only, and busi-
nesses were closing their doors. People debated whether face
masks should be required, kids e-learned at home instead of going
to school, and I waited in line for over an hour to pick up my gro-
ceries instead of shopping inside the store.

I am forever thankful that I went through my medical crisis
prior to Covid-19. It broke my heart and boiled my blood to think
of all the patients in the ICU alone during that time. Having my
family—specifically my husband, who barely left my side—with
me was crucial to my recovery. I felt so alone, and yet over and
over I was reminded I wasn't.

I remember being in my regular hospital room when I was
beginning to finally recover. The little TV in the corner of the
room was set on the news, and the newscaster talked about an out-
break in China. It felt like a faraway news story. I had a lot more to
worry about than some sickness that made people cough. I wasn't
sure I'd ever be discharged from the hospital at that point. But I

was, and it was only a month later that the pandemic truly began in America.

I still had a weak immune system. I still needed to be careful, and no one knew exactly what to expect with this fast-spreading sickness. We canceled Raylee's third birthday party at the beginning of March. No one wanted to put me at risk, but I cried a few tears knowing this would have been a party where we would have celebrated more than my daughter turning three. I would get to see my family who hadn't seen me since I left the hospital. We would celebrate that I was still a mama to Raylee as much as celebrating her turning a year older. Instead, only the four of us commemorated together with a bright pink cake. (There was a bright spot in the middle of all this darkness—how much cake I ate. I can't tell you how many slices I downed those first few months home from the hospital. So many people made or bought me cakes! I'm not complaining!)

That news story I had overheard in my hospital room was only the beginning of my constant worry. Now Covid-19 was all I heard and read about. The pandemic was *the* news story, and with it came a slew of conversation around ventilators. Covid-19 patients needed them, but there weren't enough. ICUs were overrun.

Travis and I couldn't even watch some of our favorite shows anymore for fear of triggers. The first time I tried to watch *Chicago Med*, which had been one of my favorite TV shows, a patient was told, "We need to intubate you and put you on a ventilator." The exact words I'm sure Dr. Ali told me—even though I don't hold those memories anymore. It was too much. I had to turn the show off.

But it didn't matter even if I turned the TV off, the triggers surrounded me. I once scrolled through Facebook and landed on a video that automatically showed a patient's view as they were intubated. Talk about a trigger! I don't have a memory of being intubated, but I didn't want to create one either. I scrolled quickly, but my chest ached and my throat tightened. Panic rose as my eyes grew wet. I was angry that anyone would post such a disturbing video. It didn't feel fair to those of us who had experienced this trauma firsthand.

After being released from the hospital, I had tried seeing a therapist, but it wasn't working out. Her appointment times meant I had to find childcare in the middle of the day, leave my girls when we were already feeling so much separation anxiety, and the therapist I saw didn't show any remorse for what I'd been through. The couple of times I went, I felt worse afterward. I was desperate to have a place where I could openly talk about all I was feeling, but I wanted to feel peace afterward, not turmoil. I stopped seeing that therapist. During the midst of the pandemic, I began seeing Ruth, a counselor from my church, to discuss my fears and talk through my trauma experience. Something about Ruth reminded me of my mom—maybe it was the 1980s hairstyle or how outgoing she was at making others feel welcome. Ruth was very stylish in her booties and flowy floral shirt.

Together, we read through the book *Trusting God* by Jerry Bridges. The book reminded me that God was sovereign. My whole life, I had known that but until this experience, I had never fully understood it in my heart. He controls everything, which means nothing happens to us without His permission. That doesn't necessarily mean He *caused* my trauma, but He didn't stop it from happening either.

He only allows what He can use for His glory and my good. I knew Romans 8:28 by heart: "And we know that in all things God works for the good of those who love Him, who have been called according to His purpose." However, my flesh always asks why.

"I just wish I could see the good that comes from this so it would feel worth it, so I can accept it," I said to Ruth.

"You want a reason, but sometimes we don't get one," Ruth reminded me. "Without a reason, you have to just trust."
"Ah, it always comes back to trust," I said with frustration in my tone. "The one thing I struggle with most."

I struggled with the purpose of the pain I had experienced. I would find out my story had impacted someone and felt like it was all worth it, only to hear that they didn't do anything about that impact. Then, it felt worthless to me again. What good did He bring from my suffering? How was He getting any glory from all this pain and anxiety I was facing?

But worst of all, I couldn't get past the fear of more suffering in my future. Anytime I heard the word *ventilator*, I felt like I was suffocating. I was terrified of so many scenarios from failing health to public shootings. I was scared something would take my life—even a random accident that had nothing to do with my health. My heart broke for my girls.

In one of our sessions, Ruth asked me, "What would happen if you did die? Would God take care of your girls?"

I knew the answer was yes. I knew it so strongly, but it was a matter of releasing that control of being the one to take care of them. I knew I had to surrender my babies to the One they truly belonged to. When Ruth asked me that question and I had to face the truth of the answer, it shifted something in my heart.

The fear of dying faded. I knew I would get to be with Jesus in perfect peace, and I knew Jesus would be with my babies at the same time. My children will only ever find peace in Jesus, not in me being their mama. Even if the trauma of losing their mom changed them, God could bring good from it and grow them closer to Him, which is my ultimate desire in the first place.

I believe often as moms, we hold on too tightly to our children. I am certainly guilty of this in so many ways. I have dreams for them, and I love them too much to let them take risks that could cause them any type of hurt, whether a skinned knee or a bruised heart. My love for them is so fierce and protective that I feel the only way to keep them safe is for me to control everything. To hold them in my hands. Wrapping my fingers around them and squeezing tight. But when we squeeze too tight, God can't mold them into what He wants. He can't use their hurts to turn their hearts toward Him.

When we hold something in our hands with a tight grip, it can hurt when we finally release it. Our fingers can hardly stretch out straight, and our hands ache. The same is true for letting go of the tight grip on our babies. It hurts to let them go. Our hearts ache. But if we can hold them loosely, with our palms open, listening for God's direction and allowing Him to hold them, we can keep ourselves from feeling that pain. We can let go much easier.

When we can hand our babies over to God, place them in His hands to rock them, it leaves our hands empty, which means we can hold onto something else. And that something else should be God. When our hands aren't full of other things—even something as precious as our sweet babies—we can lift them up in praise to God. We can grab hold of Him so He can guide us.

During my counseling sessions with Ruth as I recovered from my hospital stay, we talked about trusting God with anything that could happen to myself or my children. I got to a point where I was able to hold my girls with open palms, allowing God to hold them and rock them. It is a lesson I learn over and over, something I have to work on every time my fingers begin to tighten around them.

Fear always causes me to grip tightly, but when I let go, I realize I have nothing to fear in the first place. "Therefore, we may boldly say, 'The Lord is my helper; I will not be afraid. What can man do to me?'" (Hebrews 13:6, CSB)

I had learned to manage one fear, but the dreaded ventilator still haunted me. So many tears fell out of pure fear of enduring a ventilator all over again.

I remember telling Travis I wanted to change my living will. We had created wills while he was in the military. Even though we were young and healthy, it's common for military families to make sure they have everything in place in case of the unthinkable. But after what I had been through, I wanted to find a lawyer to make sure the will said that I would never go back on a ventilator. I truly felt like I would rather die than suffer that way again.

Even the word *ventilator* would cause my chest to ache and my throat to feel tight. The trauma was not only in my brain, it had also etched itself into my body. One evening, I was at a leadership meeting for a mom's group at our church. We were discussing how to adapt to the pandemic rules. We'd need to move the chairs so they would all be farther apart. Would we make everyone wear masks or keep it optional? But the conversation naturally shifted.

"I read that they are running out of ventilators," one woman said. Everyone joined in the discussion, unaware that I was being sucked back into my trauma with that one word. I felt like I was falling down a tunnel, moving farther away from everyone at the table and closer to panic. Part of me wanted to jump up and run to the bathroom, get away from the conversation. But I also felt frozen, trying to hold in all the emotion.

I looked up, making eye contact with my friend, Elizabeth. Her brown eyes showed concern. She saw me. She knew. She mouthed, "Are you okay?"

I nodded my head yes, but tears started to spill down my cheeks because I actually was not okay. I felt somewhat relieved to be seen in that moment. The concern in her eyes pulled me from my tunnel and brought me back. Everyone stopped, realizing what was going on.

Tressella, the leader of the group, realized how the conversation must have been making me feel. She raised her thin eyebrows, apologized, and stopped the conversation.

As Ruth and I read through the book *Trusting God*, during our counseling sessions, this passage genuinely spoke to me:

> *God does not willingly bring affliction or grief to us. He does not delight in causing us to experience pain or heartache. He always has a purpose for the grief He brings or allows to come into our lives. Most often we do not know what that purpose is, but it is enough to know that His infinite wisdom and perfect love have determined that the particular sorrow is best for us. God never wastes pain. He always uses it to accomplish His purpose. And His purpose is for His glory and our good. Therefore, we can trust Him when our hearts are aching or our bodies are racked with pain.* [1]

---

1   Jerry Bridges, *Trusting God* (Colorado Springs: NavPress, 2017) 95.

I wanted to rejoice in suffering. But I *knew* suffering. The pain of it, but also the growth from it. I knew suffering always brought me closer to God. I knew it made me better. It truly was for my good. He always made sure it was. But could I want to be so close to Him that I was *willing* to suffer? That I *asked* for suffering because I longed for Him more than anything?

I found comfort that Jesus—who knew what was to come and was willing to be tortured and murdered—still asked God, "My Father, if it is possible, may this cup be taken from me. Yet not as I will, but as You will" (Matthew 26:39). Even Jesus asked if there was another way.

One night, the fear of the ventilator was particularly strong. I was up in the middle of the night with Ruthi, who was then six months old. I rocked her in the big open room in the darkness. A little light shone through from the high window, casting shadows through the room. I would normally pray out loud as I rocked Ruthi, hoping my voice would comfort her and using the alone time to speak openly with God. She lay against me, drifting softly back to sleep, as tears streamed down my face. I told God exactly how incredibly scared I was of being intubated again.

"I'm scared to death of going back on a ventilator, God," I whispered into what felt like an empty room. "It's not even that I'm scared of dying. If that happened, I'd get to be with You. It's the suffering, God. I don't want to suffer anymore."

I continued but this time in my head. *But You love me. I know You love me. I know anything that happens to me is in your control. You only allow situations and suffering that can be used for my good and Your glory. I have grown so close to You because of this experience. Others have gained faith from my story.*

I thought of my dad, who had prayed out loud for what I believe was the first time in his life, as he asked God to heal me that night during the prayer vigil. A simple one-sentence prayer from one father to another. If my suffering can get my earthly father to call out to my Heavenly Father, isn't it worth it? I've spent years praying that my dad would come to know Jesus on a deeper, more real level. Don't I love my dad enough to take the pain all over again if it means he finally comes to know Jesus the way I do?

I thought of the letter I opened weeks after coming home from the hospital. It was from a friend confessing that she felt more faith, for the first time in probably a decade, because of my miraculous story. Was her renewed faith worth the torment I endured?

I'm a testimony to Your healing power, I thought. *All of this is worth it. The darkness. The despair. The physical pain. Suffering is worth it. For them because I love them, but because You love them even more. It's worth it for me to know you more. So I trust You.*

Rocking back and forth in that gray glider with my sweet baby in my arms, the walls of fear came crashing down. I whispered into the dark room, "If I need to go back on a ventilator"—tears streamed down my face—"then here I am, send me."

I released my fear at that moment as I looked up into the shadow-covered ceiling, tears dripping down off my cheeks. I surrendered my push against suffering, welcoming it, if somehow, some way, it could grow His Kingdom.

Are we willing to suffer if that's what it takes to bring people to Christ? Most of us, myself included, are so cocooned in our comfort we won't even step out into an awkward conversation to grow His Kingdom. To grow in Christ, are we willing to surrender our comfort?

That night in Ruthi's dark bedroom, I surrendered. I was willing to suffer if it meant it could bring people I loved or even people I didn't know to come to know Him. If suffering and pain could grow me as His follower, then with only enough courage to whisper, I said, "Let it be."

If that's what it takes. Anything for Him. Anything for more of Him. That whispered prayer was something I'll never forget, but it was only my first step in surrender. There was much work still to do.

CHAPTER 10

Know Your Mama

But now thus says the Lord, He who created
you, O Jacob, He who formed you, O Israel:
"Fear not, for I have redeemed you; I have
called you by name, you are mine."

Isaiah 43:1(ESV)

"You're going to know your mama," she whispered to the baby in her arms. My mom had dropped my kids off with my mother-in-law, Mary Jo, when we realized I would be in the hospital recovering from the drain they put in for my infection.

Mary Jo had brought them to Cara and Justin's house to stay. After my kids were unpacked and settled, it was time for a cousin's birthday party. But Ruthi happened to be asleep when it was time to leave, so Mary Jo offered to stay with her while she took her nap.

Mary Jo's husband, Tim, called to tell her they were transferring me to the ICU. She began to worry as she made Ruthi a bottle. She looked into those innocent blue eyes as she fed her, sitting all alone in the big empty house. Tears rolling down her cheek, she whispered to Ruthi, "You're going to know your mama."

Not long after feeding Ruthi her bottle, Mary Jo got another call from Tim. He sounded more concerned.

"They're putting her on a ventilator," he said.

Mary Jo immediately got on her knees, sobbing, and begged and pleaded with God to save me. After she prayed, she held Ruthi in her arms again, rocking her and repeating, "You're going to know your mama."

I learned about her words and prayers over my daughter from a letter she wrote to me about a year after my medical trauma. It's a letter I read about once a year to remind myself how powerful God is and that this story is more than my own. I'm someone who believes prayers don't expire. Each prayer Mary Jo prayed over that baby and her mama continues today, even as Ruthi turned five this year.

After I was discharged from the hospital, follow-up appointments with my surgeon and primary care doctor filled our calendar. Because I left the hospital with an infection still looming inside my abdomen, tests and lab work remained vital to be sure the infection was diminishing rather than growing.

Because of the sudden separation I had experienced from my kids, we all had separation anxiety. Raylee would cry, pleading, "Don't leave," and wrap herself around my leg when I walked out the door for another appointment. Once I got to the car, I broke down—crying, upset that I upset her. I worried my absence for those two weeks in the hospital had left her traumatized. I worried she'd never recover.

Then, on the drive to the doctor, anxiety would hit that something would happen to me. What if that was the last time I would ever see her? My chest got heavy and my throat tightened. It took all my composure to hold in the tears that began to seep out of my eyes.

One time, Travis and I left to go to a high school basketball game together. We needed some time together, doing something fun after months of medical discussions. I waffled on whether to go. This wasn't a necessity like a doctor's appointment, but I also craved the time with Travis. We were visiting Travis' family, and Raylee was finishing her dinner at the kitchen table with Cara's family and Mary Jo. I hesitated when it was time to say goodbye. Mary Jo could see the delay and worry in my eyes as my forehead creased. *Would Raylee understand? Would she be scared that we wouldn't come back for a long time again?*

"She will be fine," Mary Jo assured me, waving her hands at us to go ahead. "Go and have fun! It will be good for you."

I kissed Raylee and Ruthi on their foreheads and rushed out the door before I changed my mind.

As soon as we drove down the road and out of Cara's neighborhood, I began to imagine every terrible scenario. *There would be a bombing in the school. The whole place would blow up and we would die. We would never come home to Raylee. She would never be the same after such a loss.* I looked out the passenger window as we drove past fields, keeping my face turned away from Travis. I was tired of making him deal with my breakdowns, and I didn't want him to see any tears building in my eyes.

Once we got seated in the bleachers of the school, Travis went to buy a drink at the concessions. I texted my mom, feeling silly for the fear, but unable to stop the tears in the middle of this crowd of strangers. She sent me a prayer through text, and I took deep breaths until I could focus again.

This was only the beginning of the anxiety I faced after my medical trauma. Even after working through it with my counselor Ruth, even after that night where I surrendered my fears to God, even after years had gone by, the anxiety would always come back. I believe it was partly because I hadn't yet fully worked through my trauma. But ultimately, it boiled down to this: I took my focus off of God and placed it on my fears.

It reminds me of a story from the book of Exodus. The Israelites had been slaves to the Egyptians for more than four hundred years (Exodus 12:40). God sent Moses to ask Pharaoh to let the Israelites go and serve God, but Pharaoh's heart was hard, and he kept saying no. God did many signs and wonders through Moses, but it didn't matter. There was plague after awful plague upon the Egyptians: frogs in their beds, gnats in their food, boils on their skin. Yet, Pharaoh didn't waver. He was not letting his slaves go. But they weren't his people; they were God's.

In the final straw, God sent an angel of death to kill every firstborn in every Egyptian family, including the firstborn of their animals. However, God spared all the Israelites. Can you even imagine the amount of crying that night? The wailing. The fear. The loss the Egyptians awoke to the next morning was enough to finally break Pharaoh's heart, and he told Moses to go!

The Israelites were made up of around 2.4 million people—pretty much the population of Houston, Texas. Leaving Egypt with all their animals and food and whatever they wanted to take with them—it was a major move.

I've had my fair share of moves in life. By the time Travis and I had been married for six years, we had moved five times. (Yeah, I know how to pack a box or two.) I also know how incredibly stressful it can be, especially as a mama. I can't even imagine trying to move two million people at once!

The Israelites traveled by night and day into the wilderness after they were free from slavery. But Pharaoh changed his mind. He realized what he had done in letting all the slaves go. Who would do all the work now? It was as if his grief turned to anger. Pharaoh and his army gathered more than six hundred chariots and went after them. Exodus 14:10 tells us, "When Pharaoh drew near, the people of Israel lifted up their eyes, and behold, the Egyptians were marching after them, and they feared greatly." On one side was an angry army ready to come after them and on their other side was a huge body of water called the Red Sea. They were trapped, or so it seemed. When God has a plan, He doesn't desert us right in the middle of it.

He made the winds part the sea, leaving a dry path right down the middle for the Israelites to walk through all the way to the other side. After every child and donkey of the millions of Israelites had safely crossed, the Lord shifted the winds, causing the seas to crash onto every Egyptian soldier and horse. Not a single one of the six hundred chariots survived those waves.

Here's the deal: Too often we don't celebrate what God has done in our lives because we turn around and focus on the Egyptians coming after us. All we see are the chariots and the angry men and the weapons, when right in front of us God has parted the Red Sea. In our minds, we know we are free, but we don't *feel* free. We feel afraid.

We see all the tragedies, the unanswered prayers. I saw every possible way I could die—scenarios that are very unlikely to happen. But I was in tears—sometimes even panic attacks—over the fear of it. I was focused on the Egyptians behind me—all the what ifs and ways this world could harm me. It's not as if those fears aren't valid either. You can tell me how unlikely something is, and I'll tell you how an appendectomy should be a routine surgery that you recover from in two days, tops.

We live in an unpredictable world full of Egyptians coming after us. But we need to turn our eyes to the Red Sea! God makes a way. We are fully free. We can walk forward—on *dry* ground no less. Rather than stare at the Egyptians in horror, we need to fix our eyes on the God who has been faithful and focus on all the ways He has saved us before, reminding ourselves He will do it again. In Exodus 14:13-14, we read:

> And Moses said to the people, "Fear not, stand firm, and see the salvation of the Lord, which He will work for you today. For the Egyptians whom you see today, you shall never see again. The Lord will fight for you, and you have only to be silent." (ESV)

God allowed Pharaoh to show up and pursue His people, so He could show them exactly how mighty He is. He did it for their good and for His glory. That day, the Israelites saw the great power of God and they believed in Him like never before. And yet, how many times after this miracle did they doubt God? Did they begin to fear? I am so much like them. I've seen God save me from death. And yet, too many times I turn my eyes the wrong way and fear when I only need to look straight ahead at the parted sea and remember my God who is mighty to save.

Four years after my time in the ICU, I would do EMDR (Eye Movement Desensitization Reprocessing) therapy to work through the anxiety all my medical trauma had given me. Christina, my therapist, would give me these little blue plastic devices that fit inside the palms of my hands. She called them tappers. Each one was connected by cords to the remote Christina would hold. As I would bring up a memory in my mind, she would flip the switch, and the tappers would gently vibrate back and forth in my hands. When we experience trauma, those memories can get stuck, especially if not properly processed, and it can leave you in fight or flight mode.

The alternating vibration of the tappers works to activate both sides of the brain, which helps it to release the trauma and move those memories into your long-term memory bank where they belong. This targeted therapy, which sometimes has you focus your eyes on something that moves back and forth rather than use the vibrating tappers, breaks you free from that survival mode, allowing you to get back to living.

Guilt was an emotion that came up for me during this therapy. I couldn't care for my daughters while I was in the hospital, and even while home recovering there wasn't much I could do for them. For two full weeks while I was in the hospital, I was not the one feeding them, rocking them, playing with them, reading to them, or putting them to bed. It was a slow transition coming back to my motherly duties even after I came home to recover. I never got to say goodbye to them before being admitted to the hospital or explain to them what was happening or why I was leaving. I didn't get to pack their bags or make sure their caregiver knew the routines. It was all completely unlike me.

The guilt of not being there for them for those two weeks washed over me during one of our therapy sessions. As I focused on the feeling of guilt, I suddenly remembered Ruthi, who was four at that time of this particular therapy session, had randomly told me just a few days before: "God rocked me in my bed last night."

"Wow, that's so neat, Ruthi," I told her. "I bet that felt really special."

Inside, though, I was thinking, *What? How crazy is it that she is saying these exact words?* I've never told my kids that God rocked me in the ICU; although, that is the wording I use when sharing my story with adults. But for my kids, I keep it short and simple. "I was really sick, and God healed me, and now I'm all better."

As far as I know, Ruthi had never heard the idea of God rocking anyone. I told Christina about Ruthi telling me those words. She was as surprised as I was that Ruthi had used those exact words.

"It is so beautiful that God gave Ruthi those words to tell you," she said.

As we went back into the memories, all the guilt of not being there for my kids came rushing over me. And just as quickly, I saw God rocking Ruthi as a little baby in her bassinet, wearing her pink sleep sack when I could not be there. I saw Him rocking her now, in her twin "big girl bed" and her princess nightgown. I could hear God telling me that He would take care of my children even if I couldn't.

The idea of my children losing me, especially at such a young age, is one of the thoughts that kills me. I can torture myself with those thoughts—with the "what ifs" of how it would have affected them to lose their mom at such young ages. How close they were to that. How it would have changed the trajectory of their lives. Changed them as people. But God reminds me time and time again, especially right there sitting on my therapist's couch: they belong to Him first, He loves them even more than I do, and He will take care of them.

He took care of them for those two weeks, and I can trust Him to take care of them for the rest of their lives—whether I'm there or not. I felt as if I was sitting there having a full back-and-forth conversation with God, even as Christina ended the vibrating tappers and waited for me to open my eyes. It was only me and

God in that room as He reassured me my babies would always be rocked by Him.

He wasn't only holding *me* in His strong hands during that breathing test. He was holding my girls too. He was holding all of us, rocking us gently. He was keeping us safe and secure.

Fears would come up in my therapy sessions with Christina. I would immerse myself into a memory, trying to balance my mind with one foot in the memory and one foot in the present during EMDR. One particular session, my memory took me back to the urgent care when I first experienced my abdomen pain. But this time it was only for a blood draw to check my levels after another follow-up appointment following my hospital discharge.

As is typical for me, the nurse could not get the needle into my vein correctly. She stuck me with the needle multiple times as I cried. Tears from the pain but most of all from the memories and the fear. She finally gave up and told me I would need to go into the hospital to have them do the blood draw. I walked into the hallway and completely broke down. I sobbed into Travis's chest as he held me.

"I don't want to go back to the hospital," I said through gasps. "I can't go back."

It felt like I could drown in the fear of being admitted again. What if they found something wrong? What if somehow I ended up back on the ventilator? I could picture Raylee crying as we left for my appointment. I could see myself promising we wouldn't be gone long, and Mommy would be back. But now, what if I didn't come back? What would that do to her if I disappeared again? And what if this time, I didn't survive?

Tears flowed from my closed eyes as all these memories came rushing back while the tappers vibrated quickly between my hands.

"Okay, breathe," Christina said, bringing me back to the present, to her office.

I was sitting on the smooth couch, a large metal clock on the wall opposite me. I took a deep breath as I opened my eyes, forcing myself to make eye contact with her to ground myself. She had gentle eyes and asked what I had noticed. She listened intently, jotting down a note or two, as I told her what I had seen, what I had felt in the memory. My mouth was cold, and my tongue was tingling—physical reactions to the trauma.

"Okay, let's go back to that," she said, crossing her legs, one sandaled foot over the other. I closed my eyes again and felt the tappers begin to vibrate back and forth in my hands. I went back to the memory, seeing myself walking back into the hospital. My mind could no longer hear the ticking of the two clocks in the room—neither the small desk clock sitting next to me nor the big round one behind Christina. Instead, I heard quiet conversations, the automatic doors opening and closing. Travis was next to me in the hospital waiting room. But this time, I pictured Jesus there too.

Christina had taught me that I could invite Jesus into the memories, and she had told me to try it with this one. I saw us sitting in the large, open waiting area, watching people come to the front desk to check in. I saw me sitting in the chair in a tiny room as the nurse told me I have terrible veins and tried her best to draw my blood. All the visuals flashed through my mind. There was little Raylee back at the house, wondering when I'd be back. She was standing at the door looking for me.

I heard God gently say, *Remember? I'll take care of her.*

Christina reminded me that God was taking care of me too as I had my blood drawn that day. The next time we went back into the memory, I remembered that I did in fact make it home. That we had been gone so unexpectedly long that we were starving, so we stopped to grab pizza. Then we went home. I made it back to my girls, and they were okay while I was gone. Raylee had been playing with Grandma, completely unaware of how long we had been away.

It felt like the Egyptians were surrounding me when I found out I had to go back to the hospital for a blood draw. It felt like there was nothing left to do but fear for my life and the lives of my children as we sat in the waiting room. It felt like I was trapped in that little room with the nurse poking and prodding my arm.

But God whispered once again, *Turn around, my daughter. I've made a way. Take your eyes off of those Egyptians because You know that I take care of you. Raylee may be away from you right now, but she's going to know her mama.*

Raylee wouldn't be the only one knowing her mama though. Ruthi too, of course. And we were about to find out there would be a third little one too.

CHAPTER 11

My Ebenezer

You shall build an altar to the Lord your God of
uncut stones. And you shall offer burnt offerings
on it to the Lord your God, and you shall
sacrifice peace offerings and shall eat there,
and you shall rejoice before the Lord your God.

Deuteronomy 27:6-7 (ESV)

We've always wanted three kids. Travis grew up in a family of four
children—the only boy in a gaggle of girls. I grew up in a family
of two. Three children felt like the perfect middle. We liked the
idea of our children being close together in age, but we also always
wanted to give my body and my mental state time before trying
for another baby.

Ruthi was a much easier baby than Raylee (Ruthi actually
slept) so, if not for my medical crisis, we probably would have
started trying sooner than we had. Instead, we made sure my body
was fully recovered. Travis was ready for another baby before I
was. He is a fantastic father who loves to say yes to everything and
get everyone riled up with wrestling or adventures. But he's also

gentle and loving. I love the way he tells the girls how beautiful they look, really admiring their new dress or freshly braided hair.

Eventually, I felt that longing for one more baby too. There were fears that came along with it though. Was my body ready for pregnancy? Could my body handle pregnancy? Could my mental state, my emotions, handle being back in a hospital? I considered a home birth, but the fear of something going wrong ruled out that option for us.

Eventually though, the longing for another child outweighed all the fears, and I went off my birth control. At first it was more of a "let's just see what happens" phase. After a couple months, we began intentionally tracking my cycle. But each month that my dreaded period returned, I felt more worried that perhaps my body couldn't get pregnant again.

One of my ovaries had been infected and was almost surgically removed. Maybe it had been damaged. Maybe they both had. Maybe we would never have another child, never have a son like we'd always imagined. I had read that doctors don't run any tests until you've had a whole year of infertility or three miscarriages in a row. I thought that was pointless, but with that in my head, I waited and waited. By the six-month mark of trying with no success, I decided it didn't hurt to at least ask my doctor. Perhaps with my medical history, she would go ahead and check my ovaries.

Dr. Powell was kind and gentle, with big brown eyes and short brown hair. She and I had been pregnant at the same time during my last pregnancy. She had delivered Ruthi only days before having her own baby boy. She went to my church's second campus on the other side of the city. I sat on the paper covered table while she sat across from me on her stool, a large piece of abstract art hanging above her head on the wall. I explained my worries, being sure to mention that my ovary had been affected by my previous infection.

Dr. Powell assured me that if I was still having a period, especially one that was regular, that my ovaries were working. She actually had no concerns about them. That was a relief to hear, but what was even more of a relief was that she took me seriously and offered to run labs to see how all my levels were looking. It's wild how someone who absolutely loathes blood draws could be happy to hear she was going to do labs.

My results showed my thyroid levels were off. Dr. Powell recommended I go on a small dose of thyroid medications to improve them. I started the medicine, and the next month I saw the results I had been longing for. The pregnancy test read "positive."

By the time my jeans were no longer fitting, I realized that when we first began trying for this baby, I wasn't actually ready—mentally and emotionally. I still had healing to do, working through my trauma and grief. The last few months of waiting for that positive pregnancy test, I had finally been trusting in God's timing. I was putting my hope in Him rather than in a positive sign on a piece of plastic I had peed on. There was a lot of setting aside my plans and dreams and wishes, trusting that He knew better than me. I had to trust that He would take care of me, whether that meant helping me grieve a smaller than desired family or endure the exhausting newborn days.

I knew He had it all under control when I found out my due date: January 24. My birthday. The same week two years ago that I lay in that hospital bed with a ventilator, infection spreading, blood pressure dropping, body quitting. It was that week that Travis was sobbing, worldwide warriors were praying, and a miracle occurred. It would be that same week, just two years later, in that same exact hospital where I would be lying in a hospital bed again, but this time breathing on my own through contractions, birthing new life into this world. If Travis cried, it would be from pure joy instead of overwhelming sorrow.

This baby was another miracle in our story. From death, God brings life. Beauty from ashes. The old is gone. The new has come. All for my good. All for His glory. What a birthday it was going to be.

We found out the baby's gender at Ruthi's second birthday party. We had a taco themed party and called it "Taco Two-sday."

We planned to break open a taco-shaped piñata to reveal the gender of our new baby. No one knew the gender except Cara, who filled the piñata with the correct colored candy after opening the sealed envelope in our bedroom closet. Our backyard was full of so many friends and family who had come to celebrate with us, many of whom drove hours to be there. Travis swung the bat at the cardboard taco as everyone surrounded us in the yard. The taco went flying, leaving a small hole where a few candy pieces spilled out—enough that we all saw the answer laying in the grass. Blue. The candy was blue!

Travis hit the taco a few more times, picked it up, and swung it around so blue candy sprayed out everywhere. Everyone cheered and laughed. I couldn't believe it. I had told myself we were going to be a girl family. I had told myself how fun it would be and how good Travis was at being a girl dad. I think it was honestly all to keep myself from being disappointed if the candy was pink. But there it was: blue candy right in front of my eyes. We were going to have a son. I would have the little boy I had always dreamed of.

Despite the joy of finding out I was pregnant with my son, I also felt gnawing fear. I dreaded going back to that hospital. Driving past the Norton Women's and Children's Hospital, seeing the big building covered in blue and teal windows would leave me sobbing sometimes. The trauma felt so deep anytime I saw that hospital.

At the same time, I felt so strongly that I needed to deliver there. I wanted the familiarity of it. It wasn't only where my trauma had occurred, it was also where I had delivered Ruthi. But most of all, it felt like a piece of redemption to deliver life where I was almost served death.

My perspective shifted one day at church. Our small group was discussing an Ebenezer, which was an Old Testament altar, as a reminder of what God had done in a specific place. For instance, when God promised Noah never to flood the earth again, Noah built an altar and worshiped God (Genesis 8:20). Altars were places of testimony to the one true God, a place of worship where God was adored for who He is and what He had done. It was also a place of communion between God and the worshiper.

The name Ebenezer means "stone of help" and comes from 1 Samuel 7:12. Samuel was the leader of the Israelites at the time and was trying to turn the rebellious people back to God. He had asked them to rid themselves of their idols and pretend gods and turn their hearts to the One True God. Finally, they listened to him and assembled at a place called Mizpah. When their enemies, the Philistines, heard where they were, however, they came to attack them.

The Israelites were afraid and said to Samuel, "Do not stop crying out to the Lord our God for us, that He may rescue us from the hand of the Philistines" (1 Samuel 7:8). Samuel sacrificed a burnt offering to God. Verse 9 says, "He cried out to the Lord on Israel's behalf, and the Lord answered him." But the Philistines still drew near. Do you know what happened next? Thunder clapped in the sky—so loud that it threw the Philistine army into a panic, allowing the Israelites to attack, overtake, and defeat their enemies.

Samuel set up a stone afterwards and named it Ebenezer, "the Lord has helped us." This stone was now a symbol so that they could always remember what God had done for them.

Through our small group discussion, I realized I had the wrong perspective about the hospital. I had always thought of the hospital as a landmark of my grief and trauma. Yes, it was a place I had suffered greatly. But it was also the place God had healed me. A miracle had occurred there, but I was often too focused on the fear and pain of what I went through to see the hospital as a place where prayers were answered.

People had cried out to the Lord on my behalf, and He had answered them. This place with its dinging elevator noises and the smell of hand sanitizer could—or perhaps should—be my Ebenezer if I changed my mindset. I knew after this church discussion that I was meant to deliver our baby boy at that same hospital, and that I didn't need to fear it. God was taking care of it all, down to the specific timing of when he would be born.

I could drive by the hospital and instead of crying and reliving the painful memories, I could worship Him, praise Him for all He's done for me and relive the memories of healing miracles and support from all those who love us. It could be a place where I would remember. The Lord has helped us. The Lord was with us. That hospital is my Ebenezer, my place of remembrance and redemption.

PART 3

Survival

CHAPTER 12

God Has Healed

He himself bore our sins in his body on the cross, so that we might die to sins and live for righteousness; by his wounds you have been healed.

1 Peter 2:24

I have always liked alliteration. Maybe it's the writer in me, but even back in high school I loved the idea of all my children having names that started with the same letter. We were right on track with two daughters whose names both started with R. But we had set ourselves up for alliteration failure with that letter, because for the life of us, we could not agree on a boy's name that began with an R. Travis pushed for Reginald.

"We can call him Reggie, like Reggie Miller! He'll be amazing at three pointers," he said.

"I love Ryker. It sounds so masculine and strong," I recommended.

"Sounds like a prison to me." Travis shook his head no.

We finally ruled out the R names. More than alliteration, the meanings of names are the most important to me. I wanted a name that fit this miracle boy of ours. So each name we discussed, I looked up the meaning. But every name we liked had a lame meaning. Nothing was right. Nothing was good enough.

On a trip to Niagara Falls—for our babymoon—we began discussing names again. I had a list on the Notes app on my phone with names I had randomly heard or suddenly thought of that I liked. I hadn't looked any of them up yet, but we went through them, narrowing down the list. There were a couple we both liked. Travis flipped open his computer and we began looking up the meanings. He typed Josiah into the search bar. As soon as the results came up, I gasped. It read, "God has healed." What a perfect statement regarding our story.

The fact that I was carrying this new life after almost dying proved God had healed. This baby was the proof of that. He was yet another miracle in our story. Even though we said we'd consider the name Josiah and use it only between us to see if we truly liked it, I knew deep down in my heart this was his name. It had to be.

My entire pregnancy I had assumed I would be induced like I had been with Raylee and Ruthi. When it comes to labor, it's as if my body only needs a kick and then it takes over on its own. I've had fairly easy inductions compared to a lot of people. I like being induced because I can have a plan for childcare, and I know what to expect for the most part. When I got to thirty-nine weeks and Dr. Powell explained that the hospital had now changed their policy, I was taken aback.

Because the hospital was so busy, they wouldn't schedule any inductions (unless medically necessary) until you were "40+5," which landed me on a weekend. And they don't schedule inductions on weekends. That left me with the date of Jan. 31, when I would be forty-one weeks pregnant. Honestly, I was upset by this change of plans. It was unexpected. I didn't have childcare lined up that late, and I also didn't want to wait that long. By thirty-nine weeks, I knew I'd be uncomfortable, and we'd all be desperately waiting to meet the new baby.

Fast forward to the day after my due date. I went in to be checked and was three centimeters dilated. They did an ultrasound on the baby to get an estimate of his size and check on all his fluid. He was measuring big—9 lb 13 oz, with a margin of error of plus or minus one pound. He could be normal size or he could be huge.

The OB I saw that day suggested having a C-section because of the risk for shoulder dystocia with larger babies born vaginally. This upset me. It was more news I wasn't expecting, and I began to feel distressed. Now I had to make a huge decision: opt for a C-section or stick to the plan of delivering vaginally.

A C-section scared me so much. Knowing how my last surgery turned out, I wasn't ready to have another go at it. C-sections are a routine procedure, right? Well, so are appendectomies. After researching, I found that your risk for infection is higher with C-sections. Infections can lead to sepsis, and the thought of going septic again made my stomach turn sour. I also felt like a C-section was a drastic move when their measurements could be way off and shoulder dystocia, while a real risk, is also rare. At the same time, I didn't want to put my baby at risk. I needed to choose what was the safest, best option for both of us.

After talking with several people—one who has had a baby with a shoulder dystocia, many who have had C-sections, and family members who are labor and delivery nurses—I chose to stick to my plan of delivering vaginally. I did try to move my induction date up so he wouldn't grow anymore, but the hospital had no availability. I was still set for January 31.

I prayed and prayed I would go into labor on my own that week of my due date, while my mom was already there to take care of the girls. I walked a lot, even curb walked around the mall, and ate pineapple. Nothing worked.

I felt like God surely was going to have this baby come out the same week I was in the ICU. In fact, in my heart I wanted Him to write this story so that this baby was born at exactly 9:02 p.m. on January 26—the exact day and time Travis looked at the clock when God rocked me in my hospital bed. The story couldn't get better than that, right? I thought that must be God's plan. But that day came and went. I wasn't in labor at all, no matter how much sriracha I added to my dinner. I had to trust that God's timing was better than my own.

Monday, January 31 came. I called the hospital at 5 a.m., but they didn't have space for me yet. They said they would call when they were ready for me and to go about my morning normally. I had no idea if I'd be waiting a few hours or a few days. I had waited two days to be induced with Ruthi because the hospital was so full.

Thankfully, the hospital called late in the morning and said they were ready for me. They asked me to come in around 12:30 that afternoon. I had already showered and eaten breakfast. This gave us enough time to finish packing, load the car, get a snack, and talk to the girls to explain everything that was about to happen. I was so glad we got to leave while they were awake, and we could say goodbye to make sure they understood what was happening. I had been worried that if I did go into labor on my own, we would leave in the middle of the night. I didn't want to do that to them again after everything we'd been through. Plus, childcare plans had changed multiple times, so I wanted to be clear with them on who was going to be taking care of them while we were away.

Once we got to the hospital, it took a while to get situated. We got to our room, I changed into my hospital gown, and we met my nurse, Becky. She felt motherly. Right away she put my IV in, which is honestly a terrible part of having a baby, in my opinion. I warned her that everyone has trouble getting them in, and I was right. She gave up on my arm once the tears started streaming down my face and moved to try the IV in my hand.

The OB on call that day, Dr. Taylor, came in to see me too. We showed Becky and Dr. Taylor the snack basket we had made for them all, and I explained that I had previous medical trauma and hoped they would read my story, which was written out next to the snacks, to better understand all I would be dealing with while at the hospital.

The fear from being back in a hospital and the reality of all that could go wrong was so real. I knew that at any moment I could react with a panic attack or weeping or who knew what. I wanted everyone who was caring for me to understand what I had been through and be prepared for any reactions I may have.

I also thought of this as a chance to share our testimony. I wanted them all to know God hears our prayers and He heals. I knew each of them had their own story and perhaps even their own pain. I hoped my story would encourage and even witness to anyone who needed it. The snack basket eventually got taken out to the nurses' station for anyone to enjoy a treat and read my story. Becky understood and was sweet to us after reading what I had been through. Several nurses came in to thank us for the snacks and for sharing my story. One nurse even said she would be praying for me.

The OB and nurse were ready to get the show on the road. In fact, it felt a little rushed and made me nervous. Dr. Taylor couldn't wait to break my water, and as soon as the thirty minutes of monitoring was done, she got right to it! I was still only three centimeters dilated, which shocked me after all the walking I had done that week.

She broke my water, which wasn't a pleasant experience. With Raylee's birth, the nurse broke my water after the epidural was in, so I didn't feel it. With Ruthi's birth, my water broke on its own during induction. After they broke my water, they saw that he had had a bowel movement as meconium was coming out with the fluid. I got stressed and worried.

"This is very normal for someone who is forty-one weeks along," Becky assured me. "It most likely won't be an issue, but we will have extra nurses in the room during delivery to make sure he is safe."

They wanted to see if my body would take over after my water broke, but it didn't. Pitocin was started, and it wasn't long until I began to feel contractions. They started coming hard.

"Babe, just get the epidural," Travis said, hating seeing me in pain. "This isn't a contest to see how long you can last or how much pain you can endure."

Dr. Taylor had said the same thing, so I asked for the epidural.

We told the anesthesiologist that during my last epidural my blood pressure had dropped too low. He said he would "take it easy" on me to hopefully prevent that from happening again. Getting the epidural is never fun, of course, but this time it was extra scary to me. They let Travis stay in the room, but he had to sit down and let the nurse be the one to help me. Becky talked me through it all and held me. I was a sobbing mess through it, but it was mostly from the fear. Becky was so understanding and helped me through it so much.

Rather than lay me on my back, which can cause a blood pressure drop, they turned me on my side—back and forth—once the epidural was in. They checked me about thirty minutes later, and I was five centimeters dilated. My blood pressure began to drop, however, so they gave me ephedrine to help and kept turning me. With both of my previous epidurals, I had been so relaxed and numb that I was able to sleep. That was not the case with this one. Instead, I was freezing. The labor shakes had started after my epidural.

Everything felt tingly and uncomfortable. It was anything but relaxing. It did take the pain of the contractions away, but I could still feel the pressure of them. I knew when one was happening where during previous births someone had to tell me. I hoped this would help me push better. I could still wiggle my toes too, so I knew this epidural was not as strong as my others.

The nurses were a bit concerned because the baby's heart rate was having late decelerations, meaning it was dipping at the end of my contractions and not coming back up until after the contraction ended. Because of this, they had to turn off my Pitocin and insert an internal monitor to track my contractions. I was asking if something was wrong, and they did a great job of explaining it without making me worry. They were so calm the whole time, which helped me stay calm.

They decided to give me fluid through my IUPC. They explained that a lot of fluid had left my body already, leaving little room for the baby to move around. I didn't understand it fully, but they inserted fluid for the kid to swim around some more.

It was almost time for shift change. We were sad for Becky to leave, and we joked with her that she did all the hard work and now someone else was going to come in and get the credit when the baby came. Since she was about to leave, she came over and talked to me about all that was happening.

"You don't seem to be progressing, Tiffany," Becky explained, reaching out and taking my hand. "Sometimes that could mean you would need a C-section."

I could tell that she could see the fear in my eyes. She was trying to comfort and encourage me.

"I'm starting to feel a lot of pressure," I interrupted her.

She checked me and what do you know? I was complete, ten centimeters dilated! We laughed, saying my body heard her say C-section and said, "No way, Jose!"

In less than an hour, I had gone from five to ten centimeters, with my contractions coming only one minute apart. It was go time! I was excited and anxious to start pushing. It was the first time during a birth that I felt like pushing.

But we had to wait for Dr. Taylor to arrive. It was a little after 7 p.m. when she got there. Becky caught the new nurse up on everything but said she was staying to see this baby be born! I loved that, and it made me so happy that she wanted to stay to see us through. Everyone was ready. We started my push playlist, and they got a mirror in place. This was the first time I chose to use a mirror while pushing.

When they first wheeled it over, I wondered if this was such a good idea. It was a pretty disgusting view to be honest. But I knew seeing the progress would help me know when pushing was working. This was also the first time that I told everyone else when it was time to push rather than them telling me. I liked that I could feel the contractions coming so I knew when to push. There were rest times between pushes too, so it didn't feel rushed or urgent. It was by far the best pushing experience I've had.

After about five minutes of pushing, Dr. Taylor suggested doing a little cut. I told her no. I had an episiotomy with Raylee that ended in a fourth-degree tear, and I will never choose to go that route again. Plus, I had barely been given a chance to push at this point. I told her to let me keep trying, and she agreed.

Years ago, I would not have pushed back and told a doctor no. My medical trauma had taught me to use my voice more, to advocate for myself. I've learned I know my body best. It only took a total of about ten minutes, and he was out. I will never forget what it looked like seeing his head come out, knowing I probably only had one more push to get his body out. It was amazing and terrifying and gross and wonderful.

I saw the cord and then his head and worried when he wasn't immediately crying. But within a few seconds, he screamed as everyone worked to suction him and wipe him down while he lay on my chest.

Travis cut the cord as my tears came. I was overwhelmed with relief and joy. I had a son. Josiah Timothy was born at 7:19 p.m., on Monday, Jan. 31. He weighed 9 lb. 7 oz. He was born the day I had my second drain put in, only two years prior. He had a smushed face, pale skin, and a head of dark hair.

Now, he's a walking-talking-tractor-obsessed-looks-just-like-his-mama boy. Some people don't believe in miracles, but you'll never be able to convince me otherwise—not when there's one holding my hand calling me mama.

CHAPTER 13

I'm Still Here

The light shines in the darkness, and the
darkness has not overcome it.

John 1:5

It was January 2020 when I survived sepsis. But it was January 2023 that it all began to unexpectedly break me. I felt completely physically healed and recovered. Josiah was finally starting to consistently sleep through the night. We had finally made the move back to Indiana to live near family—a dream we'd had for nine years. And yet, I was finding myself angry often, and that anger was turning into rage.

Raylee was five, Ruthi was three, and Josiah would soon be one, so they had typical behaviors of disobedience and testing me. But I couldn't handle it. We all lose it sometimes, but this was different. I would scream, scaring them to hide under the table. I would slap the table and yell when they wouldn't listen. The final straw was when I slammed my fist at the wall. This wasn't me. And it for sure wasn't who I wanted to be.

I felt like I was failing my whole family. I couldn't keep myself

in control. I couldn't stay calm when they weren't calm. I was trau-
matizing them. After an episode of rage, I'd sit down and sob my
eyes out. I felt so much guilt for how I was behaving. I felt like my
kids were going to remember me as angry, someone they had to
walk on eggshells around. I was scared it would only get worse, and
I would eventually hurt one of them unintentionally.

I began to think something was wrong with me. *Perhaps my
hormones are off.* January was a hard month usually, but this one
was especially hard. Despite moving to a place I'd dreamed of, I
didn't feel settled. I still deeply missed the church and relationships I had left. We had unpacked boxes stacked in rooms, despite
living there for months. I hadn't slept through the night much in
the past year since I was breastfeeding Josiah. And he was starting
to wean, which can make your hormones fluctuate.

Because of breastfeeding and nap schedules, I hadn't felt
much freedom for the past year either. The holidays were over,
along with the busyness and magic of it all. Instead, it was now
nothing but a dreary winter. Travis was scheduled to leave for a
two-week business trip out of the country for his new job, and the
anxiety of him being gone weighed on me.

As if all that wasn't enough, it was the month of my trauma
anniversary. If my mind didn't remember, Facebook Memories
would. And if I didn't look at Facebook, it didn't matter, because
it turns out our bodies remember trauma anyway.

I had done everything I could think of to help myself. I worked
out five days a week. I read my Bible every morning while Josiah
played or ate some dry cereal sitting next to me, trying to steal
my pen as I took notes. I attended our new church regularly after
months of trying different ones. I tried so hard to stop and pray
when I was feeling impatient.

But it didn't matter what I put in place to help myself, I was at
my breaking point. The blanket of depression I once felt in that
hospital room only three years earlier had come back. But this
time it wasn't just heavy. It was wrapping itself around my face

and neck, suffocating me. I could barely see the light, grasping all over to make my way out but getting nowhere.

My best guess was my hormones, so I found doctors and made appointments to check my levels. Everything always came back normal. All my ideas for what might be wrong were not the answer. I was physically in the clear.

Somehow, I found a free service for counseling online. I set up an appointment to try it out. I did two Zoom meetings and realized I hated it. I didn't like meeting on Zoom. The therapist didn't seem to know what questions to ask me. When I did open up a little, she surprised me by giving surface-level advice rather than digging to the root of my issues.

It all felt awkward and unhelpful. However, she was able to give me an evaluation and diagnosed me with Generalized Anxiety Disorder (GAD). After researching it, I'd never read anything truer about myself. GAD is a mental health condition that causes you to experience excessive, persistent, and unrealistic worry about everyday things.

I knew I wanted to find a therapist who would help me. I began my search online and asked around for recommendations. I finally found someone who seemed to fit what I was looking for. From what I could tell online, she was a believer but also a licensed and highly trained therapist with years of experience. Her sessions were in person and only thirty minutes away from our house. The bad news was she had a six-month wait list.

In the meantime, I had been referred to a psychiatrist to get a mental health evaluation. She agreed with the GAD diagnosis and prescribed me medication to help with my anxiety. I had a lot of reservations about starting medication. I felt a stigma about taking anxiety or depression medication, especially among Christians. I was afraid of what others would think, so I didn't tell people. I was afraid they would think I just wasn't trusting God enough.

It took a few months to find the right dosage and see effects, but I found the medication kept my frustrations from turning into rage. I wasn't lying awake at night spiraling about every possible bad scenario that could hurt my children. I'm still disappointed in how long it took me to find help for myself—not because I wasn't trying, but because of what our mental health system is like. But six months into the year, I was beginning to feel more like myself. It made me wonder whether I should keep the therapy appointment I had waited so long for. I'm so glad I did.

My new therapist, Christina, was indeed a believer, and she invited Jesus into our sessions, which is what I had longed for. I immediately felt as if I could trust her. Her small tan office with its soft brown loveseat became my safe space to be real and vulnerable and even fall apart. It wasn't long before Christina introduced me to EMDR therapy.

Four months into our sessions, we began this form of therapy. For the first time, I relived my medical trauma in a way that brought healing rather than leaving me feeling broken.

My first session of EMDR was spent focusing on the most disturbing memory from my experience. That has always been the moment I was suctioned out before my breathing test. The experience was horrifying. Of all the moments I don't remember, I wished this was one of them. Instead, the memory would haunt me. I would have flashbacks for weeks of this moment, specifically the sound of it along with the feelings of fear followed by regret.

EMDR is a lot like exposure therapy because you repeat the memories in your mind over and over until they become less and less disturbing. During our therapy sessions, I would replay the memory over and over in my mind. Seeing the blue tube, feeling the pain in my throat, sensing Travis to my left, and the sound of being suctioned out. I can't describe the sound, but it was the sound of nightmares to me.

The horrifying feeling would well up in my chest right as Christina would say, "Okay," and bring me back to the present.

"Remember to keep one foot in the memory and one foot in the present," she said, making sure I never stayed in a memory too long.

It never made much sense to me how it works. I would think

that focusing on and replaying a memory over and over would make it stick with me. But somehow, with the help of those vibrating tappers, the memory began to fade and became much less intense. Eventually, I could no longer hear the suctioning sound. The relief still brings me to tears. It's as if all this time I was trying desperately not to feel the pain and once I let myself hold it and examine it—only then I was able to let go of it.

It reminds me of a quote from Aundi Kolber in her book *Try Softer*. She says, "The moment I let go of needing to control the pain as my son was being born was precisely the moment when I was able to move through, rather than feel stuck, in the pain." [1]

Surrender is releasing our grip on needing control. It's opening our hands despite the ache from holding so tight. It's walking through the suffering again as we work through it to reprocess and heal.

At the end of the therapy session, Christina did her best to fully bring me back to the present. We worked on grounding by tossing a small brown football made of foam back and forth while she asked what I was doing the rest of the day. Sometimes, she asked me to name the shapes I saw in the room.

"A circle in that picture. The frame is square. There's a rectangle on the door."

She would ask me to name five colors I see. I would name purple, blue, and orange from the books on her shelf. Then I'd look up to the artwork above her desk—yellow, pink. She would remind me to focus on what I smelled or heard when I got back to my car or even to take a walk around the block before I drove home.

Different emotions come up during this targeted therapy experience, as you replay all the images, sounds, and feelings in your mind. You actually begin to physically feel the memories with your body while your mind releases the memories. For

---

1 Kolber, Aundi, *Try Softer: A Fresh Approach to Move Us out of Anxiety, Stress, and Survival Mode—and into a Life of Connection and Joy* (Carol Stream, Tyndale Refresh, 2020), 213.

instance, I would almost feel the tube in my throat or my whole body would tense up.

My chest would tighten, or—one of the strangest parts—my mouth would get cold. Feelings I didn't even realize I had or had at the time of the memory would wash over me suddenly. At one point, I felt anger toward the nurses. *Why didn't they tell me not to be suctioned out? Why didn't they explain that I was no longer sedated and that it would be a terrible experience? Did they tell me, and I don't remember? Did they even know how awful it would be for me?* There are always questions, so many questions. Even when family can fill in the gaps of memories you've lost, there's still so much lost in between.

EMDR is exhausting for your brain. It's like a brain workout. And every time we went back to the memory of being suctioned out, it was the same images on repeat: the blue tube, the lights on the machines to my right, Travis sitting on my left, and beyond him is the door. There are glass walls and a glass door, but they are all closed. Curtains shut. I would feel an overwhelming weight in my chest. I started to get emotional.

"Okay, deep breath," Christina said during one session. I opened my eyes and looked to the floor. I forced myself to make eye contact and took in a big inhale to bring myself back to the present. I was still in the therapist's office. *I'm not really back there in the ICU room.* I was on the tan loveseat sitting next to the cream-colored pillow with the fringe around the edges.

"What did you notice this time?" she asked.

I knew the routine now. I was ready to answer.

"I saw the door," I said. "And I wanted to escape, but I couldn't." I choked up with emotion. My throat got tight, and my chest felt like a brick was on top of it. "I just felt so trapped."

"Okay, and does it make sense that you would feel that way with what's happening?" Christina asked, her eyes gentle.

"Yes. But I just," I paused. "I've never realized that I felt like that."

The next time we went back to the memory, Christina closed

her eyes so I wouldn't feel like I was being watched. She asked me to move however I felt the urge to move. In the ICU bed, especially on the ventilator, I wasn't able to move much at all. When I went back to the memory in my brain, I let my present body stand up. I had the tappers in my hand, vibrating back and forth, and I stood up imagining myself standing up from the hospital bed. I pushed my hands out in front of me, changed my posture, and rolled my neck around. It felt so good to move while picturing the ICU room all around me. The trapped feeling melted away.

At some point, when we went back to the memory, I began to wonder if there was a window in the room. I don't recall one, but it makes sense that there should have been one. Don't most hospital rooms have windows? But I don't ever remember getting to see out of one.

Christina explained that we don't change my memories, but we do get to rewrite the script a bit if it helps us reprocess our trauma. She told me I could picture a window in the room in my memory. I could put one there myself. So I did. I went back to the memory, and I pictured a window. And this time, when I did the breathing test for an hour, instead of staring at the ceiling or closing my eyes to continue spinning in circles, I looked at the window. I saw the bluish white sky. I watched as clouds went by. I felt a bit of relief. Again, the trapped feeling melted away a little more.

During one of our sessions, Christina and I worked through the memories of the breathing test and what it felt like when I came off the ventilator.

"When we are believers, it means we get to invite Jesus into these memories," Christina said. "If you want, when you go back into the memory this time, invite Jesus to be there with you."

I nodded my head and closed my eyes. The tappers began vibrating in my hands. I saw myself sitting in the ICU room with Travis next to me. There was a nurse in the room too, but I didn't know her and couldn't even see her well. I felt confused, and a darkness weighed heavy on me. It's hard to explain, but a Bible passage talks about the plagues in Egypt when Moses asked Pharaoh to release the Israelites from slavery. Pharaoh did not want to obey God and kept answering no, so God kept sending signs to show His power and try to change Pharaoh's heart and mind. One of the plagues was darkness.

It says, "Then the Lord said to Moses, 'Stretch out your hand toward the sky so that darkness spreads over Egypt—darkness that can be felt'" (Exodus 10:21). When I heard that verse, it made my heart sink because that's what it was like—a heavy darkness, so dark you can feel it on the inside, like a depression. I felt so alone, even with people right there in the room. Even as family members came in to see me. They were all so happy to see me, so overjoyed for me to be off the ventilator. And yet, for me, I'd never felt so little joy.

As I was watching myself in this memory, I asked Jesus to come be with me.

I feel so alone, so scared, so sad. Can you come and be with me? I said in my mind.

In the memory, I saw Him this time. He walked toward me as I sat there in my hospital gown, monitors beeping all around me. My memory flashed back to when I was on the ventilator doing the breathing test. How I pictured myself curled up in the palms of His hands. How I felt Him with me. How now I know He rocked me in the ICU that night and healed me.

My brain went back to the original memory of me sitting in the room, fresh off the ventilator, feeling nothing but despair. I saw Jesus bending down as I sat there surrounded by darkness, feeling buried in it. He squeezed my hands, and I heard him softly say, "I'm still here. I've never left."

A relief washed over me, and tears ran down my face like a flowing river as I opened my eyes to Christina sitting across from me in her big black desk chair.

He was there the whole time. He hadn't left. I wasn't alone. No matter how dark it felt, the Light was with me. A light that never goes out no matter how heavy the darkness is.

CHAPTER 14

Bring It On

Therefore, if anyone is in Christ, he is a new
creation; the old has passed away, and see, the
new has come!

2 Corinthians 5:17 (CSB)

Almost four years after my time in the ICU, Travis and I sat at
the table for two in the corner of a candlelit stone restaurant. We
devoured pasta and sipped wine while the owner who was known
for being "crazy" walked around telling everyone he loved them
and offering them a bite of fresh shaved meat. We were on our
dream trip to Italy, tucked inside a Michelin star restaurant in the
city I'd always wanted to visit: Cortona.

Ever since I met Travis, he's had this passion for helping me
mark the items off my bucket list–a list I wrote up in college. It
includes items like seeing a monkey in the wild, riding on the
back of a motorcycle, getting married, and running a 5K. Travis
loves traveling and adventure, which reminds me of my grandma
who used to take me on "adventure days" when I was little. When
I graduated college, Travis took me on a hot air balloon ride to

celebrate—marking that item off my list. When we were first married, we planned an excursion to swim with dolphins on a stop on our cruise—mark that off my list!

My biggest dream was to take a romantic trip to Italy with my husband someday. He made it happen for our ten-year anniversary. It was a lot of planning and saving money, but we knew more than ever that our days were numbered and now is the time to fully live our lives.

It felt so full circle as we got comfortable on our first flight—well, as comfortable as you can be in the back row of an airplane. I wasn't picturing the plane crashing and my babies crying for the mama they'd never see again. I wasn't crying through a panic attack as the plane took off. I trusted that my babies were in good hands—the relatives we trusted them with, but ultimately a God I can trust. I wasn't shaken by the worries. I was solid in my peace.

We spent two weeks traveling through Italy, starting in Venice and exploring the canals. Our favorite part of the trip was driving through Tuscany, staying at a resort that treated us like royalty, and taking a personal cooking class from a local woman who taught us how to make fresh pasta and then sat down to enjoy it with us.

We climbed the steps up the Amalfi Coast and swam in the refreshing sea, only getting out to nibble on our bright red tomatoes on top of our bruschetta. We finished our trip in Rome, taking all the tours and reveling in the ancient architecture with the large columns and grand wooden doors on so many buildings. It was the trip of a lifetime for us. I don't know that we will ever be able to top it. But I know that we will try.

Experiencing suffering, whether it be in the grief of loss and unanswered prayer, or in the physical and mental suffering of trauma, changes us. It shifts our perspective. Our days are numbered, and because we don't know that number, we should be living each day with gratitude and purpose and joy.

Now is our time to live. I don't want to put off my dreams any longer than necessary. Hence, writing the book I've always wanted to publish! But I also don't want to put off my purpose. God didn't save me so I could lick gelato overlooking the Tuscan sunflower fields. Although, I know He delights in seeing me experience that.

He has a purpose for my life. Now, I don't believe it's some exact career path or specific talent we have to use to serve Him. I think we have many different callings all throughout the many different seasons of our lives. As Mike Donehey says in his book, "I've come to believe that God is much less interested in what we do with our lives and much more concerned with how and why we live our lives."[1]

One of the things that's become a priority to me on how I live my life is exercising. I think of how important it is to keep my body healthy after all it's been through. I know how important it is to work on my breathing, endurance, and strength in case I would ever find myself fighting for my life again. Don't get me wrong; I'm not as in shape as this makes me sound. I go through phases of not working out because I don't have the time or motivation.

But when I am in a season of regular exercise, it's because I don't want to take my body and its abilities for granted. There are too many others who have endured sepsis who must relearn how to walk, who no longer have hands to hold weights, or who never survived at all. Sometimes, I work out for them. Sometimes, I can't stop thanking God that I can breathe on my own. He has asked us all to take care of our bodies. First Corinthians 6:19-20 says, "Do you not know that your bodies are temples of the Holy Spirit, who is in you, whom you have received from God? You are not your own; you were bought at a price. Therefore, honor God with your bodies."

All of our bodies are worth taking care of–even our brains. God had physically healed me from sepsis, and my recovery was short compared to most. But He wanted to walk with me through a longer process when it came to healing me on a psychological level. That January when I began seeking help through medication and therapy was the start of another healing journey. Taking

1   Donehey, Mike, *Finding God's Life for My Will: His Presence is the Plan* (Colorado Springs, Waterbrook, 2019), 3.

better care of my body, both physically and mentally, is just one of the lessons I learned from my near-death experience.

My surgeon was correct that day he told me it would be months before I felt like myself again. It did take me months to physically recover. But I imagine he didn't have my mental recovery in mind. That would take me much longer. Why weren't there procedures in place to get me the mental help I needed during recovery? Why was I not told about the aftereffects of the trauma I experienced? There are in-person support groups, virtual support groups, websites with information on what to expect. Why didn't a single person in that hospital tell me there was help for me? Why isn't mental health as important as physical health?

Sometimes construction takes so long that we think the roads should have been left the way they were. It was hard work finding my way out of the construction zone of mental and emotional healing.

There were times the detours caused me to get lost. Times it didn't feel worth it for what lay ahead. I can't count how many times the thought *I wish I had just died* crossed my mind. Like the time I lay in our bedroom closet, my body clumped into a heap on the floor as everything in my life, in the world, felt too heavy.

When all the big orange barrels are finally taken down and the brand new, smooth lanes are all open, we realize how worth it the construction was. The drive is now easier and faster and smoother. Even though the construction period is over, it doesn't mean the road stays brand new. There will come times where a pothole needs to be filled.

This is true of trauma as well. We can do the hard work and get to the other side with new pavement, but there will still be triggers. There will still be times where more work is needed. It's like when I drove Ruthi to her preschool and found another road closed during a massive construction project in our town.

"What needs to be fixed, Mommy?" Ruthi asked. "What's broken?"

"Well, sometimes there's construction because something is

broken and needs to be fixed. But other times there's not really anything broken, just something that can be improved or made better," I said. "They just want to make this road even better than it was. I don't think there was anything broken there."

I think about this often when I go to therapy. There are parts of me that are broken, and therapy is like the construction work mending me back together. But there are also parts of me that aren't broken but could use improving. Therapy is that type of construction too. Both types are worth the new that comes when all the work is finished. But for me, there is always more work to do—mainly, the work of surrender.

It's the work of letting go of the need for control, of loosening my grip, of taking a step back instead of hovering over. It's raising my children to know and love the Lord, but knowing ultimately their salvation is not up to me.

I used to pray that my children would be protected, safe, and healthy. I would pray that they would never have their hearts broken and never experience tragedy. But through my suffering, I've learned there is no stopping this cruel world from hurting my children. I know, someday, they will have their hearts crushed, they will experience tragedy, they will know loss. None of us can escape it. No matter how much I try to protect them or even pray over them, they will not be immune to this fallen world.

I still pray for their protection and health, of course, and I do believe those prayers are heard and often answered. But my prayers have grown more mature as I have grown more mature in my faith. Now, I pray that *when* the inevitable hurts of the world come for my children that they will lean into God rather than push Him away. I pray that their broken hearts or broken bodies will become stronger *because of* their suffering, that their foundations that I'm helping build now will never crumble, no matter how much they are rocked by earthquakes. That their wrestling will mold them into golden warriors for God.

Could we as mamas ever get to a place where we are more concerned for our hearts, souls, and eternities than we are for our comfort, health, and things of this earth? I don't believe God expects us to come to that place for our own children, and maybe not even for ourselves, because He knows we are merely human. But what a level of sanctification if we did get to that place, what a place to strive for. I want to get to the place where knowing Jesus and being more like Jesus is so crucial to me that I can say to suffering, "Bring it on. Send me." I want to lay down my push against pain, to give up my clinging to comfort. I want to surrender, because I desperately need surrender. I want to welcome whatever it takes to be as much like Jesus as possible.

I pray that Raylee, Ruthi, and Josiah grow so close to Jesus that he becomes as familiar as their favorite soft blanket, that the slightest touch from Him would wash them in relief and reassurance. We can pray that God would cradle and rock our children when they are hurting, comforting them in a way that only a loving parent can.

We can pray that these babies of ours will look more like Jesus after they walk through the fire, because we know that through the fire we are molded and changed for the better. We can pray that they will be purified like gold through their suffering. And maybe, just maybe, we can get to a place where we say, "Whatever it takes, God. Even suffering. Bring it on. Because their souls are what's most important."

It will sound cruel to the secular world. But only those of us who have walked through suffering and realized we have never left His hands will understand the importance of those prayers. We know we can trust Him in joy and sorrow, in pleasure and suffering, in healing and unanswered prayer. We can trust Him in both life and death.

Sometimes He rocks us to our core, giving us the chance to grow stronger. And sometimes He rocks us to comfort and heal us. He's the same loving God in both cases and knowing that allows us to surrender to the suffering and trust ourselves and our babies in His hands.

Acknowledgments

I never would have written this book without all the love and support of so many people. Thank you to everyone who encouraged me along the way, who watched my kids so I could go write, and who asked, "How is the book coming?" with excitement in their eyes. You pushed me to keep going when I felt like I couldn't. A big thank you to everyone on my book launch team—we did it!

To Travis, there are too many words. Thank you for standing by my side every minute of that hospital stay and being my advocate when I desperately needed one. Thank you for listening and being so understanding through all my fears and anxieties. Thank you for holding me through the tears and questions of our first loss. Thank you for your nonstop support in believing in this book and this story. And thank you for all the adventures.

To my mom, thank you for helping build my foundation in Christ. Thank you for the countless prayers for my health and wellbeing, but most of all for my soul. Thank you for all your support and encouragement in writing this book. You are my biggest fan, and your applause drowns out the insecurities.

To Raylee and Ruthi, my sweet girls—I am praying that I can help build solid foundations of faith in your hearts so that no matter what this world brings, you will be able to stand (Ephesians 6:13). I hope you will always know your mama loves you and is always here for you no matter what. I will be forever grateful that I still get to be your mama and watch you grow into beautiful girls.

Josiah, what a blessing you are to my life. I am so thankful God gave me you. It's a miracle that I'm still here, so it's like a double miracle that you are! I'm praying that you will become a warrior for God, fighting for His kingdom.

Thank you to my Hospital Angel, whoever you are. I wish I could find you and write you a letter to tell you what a difference you made in my life. Thank you for listening to me when no one else would. Thank you for caring for the whole patient.

To all the doctors, nurses, and medical staff I've encountered throughout these past eight years—thank you for caring for me and helping me heal and recover and overcome. Thank you to Alicia Laughlin, Dr. Kira Powell, Paige, Dr. Ali, Bailey, Becky, and that one guy who was the only one who could ever take my blood easily.

Thank you so much to each and every one of you who prayed for me while I was in the hospital. Your prayers were heard and answered. You were a part of this miracle. You are a part of this story. A special thank you to Aunt Rhonda for starting the prayer vigil.

Thank you to my therapist, Christina Smith, for giving me a space to be vulnerable and walking with me through so many memories. Thank you for teaching me about my brain, introducing me to EMDR, and allowing Jesus to run our sessions. Your work changes lives.

To my beta readers, Katy Betz, Sara Herrington, Lily Moreland, and Christina Post—thank you for taking the time to read through one of my first drafts and providing me so much helpful feedback.

To everyone behind the scenes who helped turn my manuscript into an actual book—thank you to Caryn Rivadeneira for your editing and Christian Rafetto for your beautiful artwork and the way you brought my vision to life. Thank you, Mindy Harvey, for helping me with branding and designing a website. A special thank you to Mikaela Mathews for coaching me through many aspects of this journey and for editing my book. You were a big encouragement to me and taught me so much along the way.

When it comes to sepsis, remember
IT'S ABOUT TIME™. Watch for:

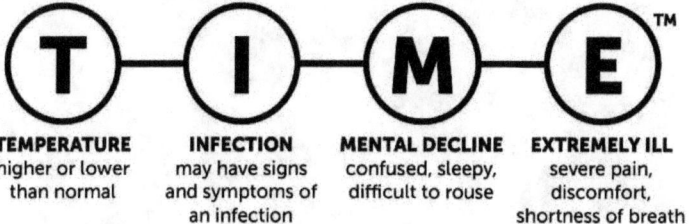

TEMPERATURE
higher or lower
than normal

INFECTION
may have signs
and symptoms of
an infection

MENTAL DECLINE
confused, sleepy,
difficult to rouse

EXTREMELY ILL
severe pain,
discomfort,
shortness of breath

If you experience a combination of these symptoms: seek urgent medical care,
call 911, or go to the hospital with an advocate. Ask: **"Could it be sepsis?"**

©2020 Sepsis Alliance   sepsis.org    **SEPSIS** ALLIANCE

For more information about sepsis or post-sepsis syndrome,
visit Sepsis Alliance at Sepsis.org.